PENGUIN BOOKS

A VOYAGE ROUND MY FATHER
THE DOCK BRIEF
WHAT SHALL WE TELL CAROLINE?

John Mortimer is a playwright, a novelist and a former practising lawyer and Q.C. During the war he worked with the
Crown Film Unit and published a number of novels before
turning to the theatre with such plays as *The Dock Brief*, *The
Wrong Side of the Park* and *Voyage Round My Father*. He has
written many film scripts, radio plays and television plays,
including six plays on the life of Shakespeare, the Rumpole
plays, which won him the British Academy Writer of the
Year Award, and the adaptation of Evelyn Waugh's *Brides-
head Revisited*. His translations of Feydeau have been per-
formed at the National Theatre and are published in Penguin
as *Three Boulevard Farces*.

Penguin published his collection of stories *Rumpole of the
Bailey*, *The Trials of Rumpole*, *Rumpole's Return*, *Rumpole for
the Defence* and *Rumpole and the Golden Thread* as well as The
First Rumpole Omnibus. Two volumes of John Mortimer's
plays, his acclaimed autobiography *Clinging to the Wreckage*,
which won the *Yorkshire Post* Book of the Year Award, and
In Character, a series of interviews with some of the most
prominent men and women of our time, are also published
by Penguin as is his most recent novel, *Paradise Postponed* –
now a major television drama series.

John Mortimer lives with his wife and their two daughters
in what was once his father's house in the Chilterns.

JOHN MORTIMER

A Voyage Round
My Father

The Dock Brief

What Shall
We Tell Caroline?

PENGUIN BOOKS

Penguin Books Ltd, Harmondsworth, Middlesex, England
Viking Penguin Inc., 40 West 23rd Street, New York, New York 10010, U.S.A.
Penguin Books Australia Ltd, Ringwood, Victoria, Australia
Penguin Books Canada Limited, 2801 John Street, Markham, Ontario, Canada L3R 1B4
Penguin Books (N.Z.) Ltd, 182–190 Wairau Road, Auckland 10, New Zealand

A Voyage Round My Father first published in Great Britain by
Methuen & Co. Ltd 1971
The Dock Brief first published in Great Britain by
Elek Books Ltd 1958
What Shall We Tell Caroline? first published in Great Britain by
Elek Books Ltd 1958
This collection first published in Penguin Books 1982
Reprinted 1983 1985, 1986

Made and printed in Great Britain by
Hazell Watson & Viney Limited,
Member of the BPCC Group,
Aylesbury, Bucks

CONTENTS

A VOYAGE ROUND MY FATHER
7

THE DOCK BRIEF
91

WHAT SHALL WE TELL CAROLINE?
133

A Voyage Round My Father

The first version of *A Voyage Round My Father* was presented at
the Greenwich Theatre in 1970. This final version of the play was
first presented at the Haymarket Theatre in August 1971 with the
following cast:

FATHER	*Alec Guinness*
MOTHER	*Leueen MacGrath*
SON (*grown up*)	*Jeremy Brett*
ELIZABETH	*Nicola Pagett*
SON (*as a boy*) FIRST BOY	*Jason Kemp*
REIGATE SECOND BOY	*Jeremy Burring*
IRIS GIRL	*Melanie Wallace*
HEADMASTER GEORGE	*Jack May*
HAM BOUSTEAD SPARKS MR MORROW	*Mark Kingston*
LADY VISITOR MATRON MISS COX DORIS SOCIAL WORKER	*Phyllida Law*
MRS REIGATE MISS BAKER FIRST ATS GIRL WITNESS	*Rhoda Lewis*
RINGER LEAN MR THONG FILM DIRECTOR	*Andrew Sachs*

JAPHET
FIRST JUDGE
SECOND JUDGE ⎫
CHIPPY ⎬ *Richard Fraser*
DOCTOR ⎭
SECOND ATS GIRL   *Tilly Tremayne*
REIGATE'S FATHER
ROBING ROOM MAN

Directed by Ronald Eyre

ACT ONE

The stage is bare except for a table and three chairs, downstage left, which are either indoor or outdoor furniture, and a bench downstage right. There is also some foliage downstage, suggestive of a garden: in particular, inverted flowerpots on sticks to act as earwig traps. This setting is permanent: changes of lighting only indicate the changes of place. The FATHER *and the* SON *(grown up) enter.*

FATHER. Roses . . . not much of a show of roses.

SON (*grown up*). Not bad.

FATHER. Onions . . . hardly a bumper crop would you say?

SON (*grown up*). I suppose not.

The FATHER, *a man in his sixties, wearing a darned tweed suit, a damaged straw hat and carrying a clouded malacca walking stick is, with blind eyes, inspecting his garden. His hand is on the arm of the* SON. *They move together about the garden during the following dialogue.*

FATHER. Earwigs at the dahlias. You remember, when you were a boy, you remember our great slaughter of earwigs?

SON. I remember.

FATHER. You see the dahlias?

SON. Yes.

FATHER. Describe them for me. Paint me the picture . . .

SON. Well, they're red . . . and yellow. And blowsy . . .

FATHER (*puzzled*). Blowsy?

SON. They look sort of over-ripe. Middle-aged . . .

FATHER. Earwig traps in place, are they?

SON. They're in place.

He leaves the FATHER, *fetches a camp stool, puts it up, guides the* FATHER *to sit down on it beside a plant.*

FATHER. When you were a boy, we often bagged a hundred ear-wigs in a single foray! Do you remember?

SON. I remember.

The SON *moves away from the* FATHER *and speaks to the audience.*

My father wasn't always blind . . .

The FATHER *starts to tie up the plant, expertly and with neat fingers. He can obviously see.*

The three of us lived in a small house surrounded, as if for protection, by an enormous garden.

The MOTHER *enters carrying a camp stool. She puts it down beside the* FATHER *and starts to help him tie up the plant.*

He was driven to the station, where he caught a train to London and the Law Courts, to his work as a barrister in a great hearse-like motor which he would no more have thought of replacing every year than he would have accepted a different kind of suit or a new gardening hat. As soon as possible he returned to the safety of the dahlias, the ritual of the evening earwig hunt.

A LADY VISITOR *appears on the side of the stage, waves to the* FATHER *who goes into hiding, moving his stool behind the plant he is tending, peers out anxiously.*

SON. Visitors were rare and, if spotted – calling from the gate – my father would move deeper into the foliage until the danger was past.

The LADY VISITOR, *frustrated, withdraws. During the follow-ing speech, the* FATHER *moves his stool back into its former position.*

Those were the days when my father could see . . . before I went away to school. When it was always a hot afternoon and a girl called Iris taught me to whistle.

FATHER. Where's the boy got to?
MOTHER. Disappeared, apparently.

The SON *(as a boy) and a small girl,* IRIS, *come running on chasing each other. In a corner the* SON *(as a boy) kneels in front of* IRIS *who is sitting neatly as she gives him a whistling lesson. The boy is blowing but no sound emerges.*

FATHER. He's running wild!
IRIS. Stick out your lips. Stick them out far. Go on. Further than that. Much further. Now blow. Not too hard. Blow gently. Gently now. Don't laugh. Take it seriously. Blow!

Sound of a whistle.

BOY. What was that?
IRIS. What do you mean – what was that?
BOY. Someone whistled.
IRIS. It was you.
BOY. Me?
IRIS. It was you whistling!
BOY. I can do it! I know how to do it!
IRIS. Well, you've learnt something . . .
FATHER. I said – the boy's probably running wild.
MOTHER. Oh, I don't think so.

In his corner with IRIS *the* BOY *manages another whistle. They chatter quietly together during the following scene.*

FATHER. Oh yes he is. And a good thing too. When I was a young boy in Africa, they sent me off – all by myself – to a small hotel up country to run wild for three months. I took my birthday cake with me and kept it under my bed. I well remember . . . (*He laughs.*) . . when my birthday came round I took the cake out, sat on my bed, and ate it. That was my celebration!
MOTHER. He'll soon be going away to school . . .
FATHER. What did you say?

MOTHER. He'll be going away to school . . . We can't expect him to stay here . . . for ever . . .

She gets up, folds her camp stool and leaves with it.
A light change. Bright sun through leaves. The FATHER *gets a step ladder and starts to walk up it, singing to himself.*

FATHER (*singing*).
'She was as bee . . . eautiful as a butterfly
And as proud as a queen
Was pretty little Polly Perkins of Paddington
Green . . .'

SON (*grown up*). One day he bought a ladder for pruning the apple trees. He hit his head on the branch of a tree and the retinas left the balls of his eyes.

Sudden, total BLACKOUT *in which we hear the* SON'S *voice.*

SON'S VOICE (*grown up*). That's the way I looked to my father from childhood upwards. That's how my wife and his grand-children looked . . . My father was blind but we never mentioned it.

The lights fade up slowly to reveal the FATHER, MOTHER, *and* SON *(as a boy sitting round a breakfast table. The* FATHER *is clearly totally blind, the* MOTHER *is helping him cut up his toast, guiding his hand as he eats a boiled egg.*

SON (*grown up*). He had a great disinclination to mention anything unpleasant. What was that? Courage, cowardice, indifference or caring too completely? Why didn't he blaspheme, beat his brains against the pitch black sitting room walls? Why didn't he curse God? He had a great capacity for rage – but never at the Universe.

The SON *(grown up) goes. The family eat in silence until the* FATHER *suddenly bursts out.*

FATHER. Take it away! This plate's stone cold! My egg! It's

bloody runny! It's in a nauseating condition! What do you want to do? Choke me to death? (*shouts*) Have you all gone *mad*? Am I totally surrounded by *cretins*?

Another silence while they go on eating.

FATHER (*singing*).
    'He asked her for to marry him
    She said "You're very kind"
    But to marry of a milkman
    She didn't feel inclined.
    But when she got married,
    That hard-hearted girl,
    It wasn't to a Viscount,
    It wasn't to an Earl,
    It wasn't to a Marquis,
    But a shade or two WUS!
    'Twas to the bow-legged conductor
    Of a twopenny bus!'

MOTHER. Marmalade, dear?
FATHER. Thank you.

Silence.

The evolution of the horse was certainly a most tortuous process. None of your seven day nonsense! Seven days' labour wouldn't evolve one primitive earth worm.

Nobody says anything.

FATHER (*singing very loudly*).
    'She was as beautiful as a butterfly,
     and as proud as a queen
    Was pretty little Polly Perkins of
     Paddington Green!'

Silence.

Is the boy still here?

MOTHER. Please, dear. Don't be tactless . . .

FATHER. I thought he'd gone away to school.

MOTHER. *Pas avant le garçon.*

FATHER. What?

MOTHER. He doesn't like it mentioned.

FATHER. Well he's either going away or he's not. I'm entitled to know. If he's here this evening he can help me out with the earwigs.

MOTHER (*confidential whisper to the* FATHER). Mr Lean's going to drive him. A trois heures et demi.

FATHER. Half past three, eh?

MOTHER. Yes, dear. Mr. Lean's going to drive him.

FATHER (*to* BOY). You'll learn to construct an equilateral triangle and the Latin word for parsley. Totally useless information . . .

MOTHER. We really ought not to depress the boy. (*to* SON) You'll find the French very useful.

FATHER. What on earth for?

MOTHER. Going to France.

FATHER. What's he want to go to France for? There's plenty to do in the garden.

As she guides his hand to the coffee.

The coffee's frozen! (*Drinks.*) Like arctic mud!

MOTHER, *takes no notice, pours him some more coffee, meanwhile trying to cheer the* BOY *up.*

MOTHER. The school's very modern. It seems that some of the older boys do sketching at weekends. From nature! I used to bicycle out with my sketching pad, from the college of art . . . I enjoyed it so much.

FATHER. All education's perfectly useless. But it fills in the *time*! The boy can't sit around here all day until he gets old enough for marriage. He can't sit around – doing the crossword.

MOTHER (*laughing*). Married! Plenty of time to think of that when he's learned to keep his bedroom tidy. (*Pause.*) The headmaster seemed rather charming.

FATHER. No one ever got a word of sense out of a schoolmaster! If they *knew* anything they'd be out doing it. (*to the* BOY.) That'll be your misfortune for the next ten years. To be constantly rubbing up against second rate minds.

MOTHER. At the start of each term apparently the new boys get a little speech of welcome.

FATHER. Ignore that! Particularly if they offer you advice on the subject of life. At a pinch you may take their word on equilateral hexagons . . . but remember! Life's a closed book to schoolmasters.

MOTHER. We'll finish your trunk this afternoon.

FATHER. You won't expect any advice from me, will you? All advice's perfectly useless . . .

MOTHER. I've still got to mark your hockey stick.

FATHER. You're alone in the world, remember. No one can tell you what to do about it.

The BOY *starts to cry.*

What's the matter with the boy?

MOTHER (*apparently incredulous*). He's not crying!

FATHER (*coming out with some advice at last*). Say the word 'rats'. No one can cry when they're saying the word 'rats'. (*Pause.*) It has to do with the muscles of the face.

BOY (*trying to stop himself crying*). Rats.

The lights fade on the breakfast table. The FATHER, MOTHER *and* BOY *go. The* SON (*grown up*) *comes to the edge of the stage.*

SON (*grown up*). Mr Ringer Lean was an ex-jockey who drove my father's antique Morris Oxford. He treated it as though it were a nervous stallion.

RINGER LEAN *enters downstage right, carrying a school trunk on his shoulder.*

RINGER. Car's lazy today. Going don't suit her. Shit scared are you? Being sent away ...

The SON *(as a boy) comes on to the stage. He is wearing school uniform, carrying a suitcase and looking extremely depressed.*

SON *(grown up).* I was to be prepared for life. Complete with house shoes, gym shoes, football boots, shirts grey, shirts white, Bulldog Drummond, mint humbugs, boxing gloves, sponge bags, and my seating plans for all the London Theatres ...

BOY. Yes.

He puts down the trunk, rests on it.

RINGER. They sent me away when I was your age. Newmarket Heath. Bound as a stable lad. Bloody terrified I was, at your age ...

BOY. Were you?

RINGER. They shouldn't send you away. You're going to develop too tall for a jockey.

BOY. I don't think they want me to be a jockey ...

RINGER. Broke a few bones, I did – first they sent me away. Ribs fractured. Collar bone smashed. Pelvis pounded to pieces. Bad mounts ... Bad Governors ... When a Governor gets after you, you want to know ...

BOY. What?

RINGER. Get to the hay loft, and pull the ladder up after you. They can't climb. Recall that. Governors can't climb. Often I've hid up the hay loft one, two, three hours sometimes. Till the Governor got a winner, and change of heart. Slept up there often. All right when the rats don't nip you.

BOY. Thanks.

RINGER. Only advice I got to give you ... never avoid a mount. Lad at our stable avoided a half broken two year old. Nasty tempered one with a duff eye. This lad was so shit scared to ride it, that you know what he did?

BOY. No . . .

RINGER. Nobbled himself with a blunt razor blade. Severed a tendon. Then gangrene. Lad had to kiss his leg goodbye.

> RINGER LEAN *picks up the trunk. He and the* SON (*as a boy*) *walk off down stage left.*

> *The light changes, coming up upstage where the* HEADMASTER, *with long white hair, a gown and a stiff collar, is standing ready to address the boys – beside him is the school* MATRON *in uniform, and a young master,* JAPHET, *with a tie tied in a wide knot and an elegant, man-of-the world appearance.*

> RINGER LEAN *and the* SON (*as a boy*) *re-enter downstage right with luggage, and cross the stage.*

BOY. It's not really a stable . . .

RINGER. So never try and nobble yourself. That's my advice. Or sterilize the blade. Hold it in a flame. Kill the germs on it!

BOY. It's more a school than a stable . . .

RINGER. Wherever there's lads, I expect it's much the same . . .

SON (*grown up*). My father had warned me – But this was a great deal worse than I'd expected.

> RINGER LEAN *and the* SON (*as a boy*) *go off.*

HEADMASTER. Now, new boys. Stand up now. Let me look at you. Some day, some long distant day, you will be one yearers, and then two yearers, and then three yearers. You will go away, and you will write letters, and I shall try hard to remember you. Then you'll be old boys. Old Cliffhangers. O.C.'s you shall become, and the fruit of your loins shall attend the School by the Water. Leave the room the boy who laughed. The fruit of your loins shall return and stand here, even as you stand here. And we shall teach them. We shall give them sound advice. So the hungry generations of boys shall learn not to eat peas with their knives, or butter their hair, or clean their finger nails with bus tickets. You shall be taught to wash and bowl straight and wipe your dirty noses. When you are in the sixth form you shall see something of golf. You will look on the staff as your friends. At all times you will call us by nick-names. I am Noah. My wife is Mrs Noah. You are the animals. My son Lance is Shem. Mr Pearce and Mr Box are Ham and Japhet. Matey is Matey. Mr Bingo Ollard is Mr Bingo Ollard. These mysteries have I expounded to you, oh litter of runts.

Pause. The lights change as the HEADMASTER, MATEY *and* JAPHET *leave.* HAM *moves to where a blackboard and a desk are set at a corner of the stage, together with two classroom chairs. He starts drawing a right-angled triangle on the blackboard.*

SON (*grown up, to the audience*). The masters who taught us still suffered from shell shock and battle fatigue. Some had shrapnel lodged in their bodies and the classroom would turn, only too easily, into another Passchendaele.

The SON (*as a boy*) *and another boy of his own age, named* REIGATE, *cross the stage and sit on the chairs in front of* HAM'S *blackboard, watching him complete his drawing of Pythagoras' theorem.*

HAM. The square on the longest side of a right angled bloody triangle is . . . is what, Boy?

Standing up in front of the desk, the BOY *says.*

BOY. I don't know . . .

HAM (*suddenly yells*). Straff you, Boy. Bomb and howitzer and straff the living daylights out of you. God bomb you to hell!

HAM *picks up the first pile of books and starts to throw them at the* BOY *one by one, shouting.*

Get your tin hat on . . . ! It's coming over now! (*Throws a book.*) It's equal to the square . . . What square, you unfortunate cretin?! (*Throws a book.*) On the other two sides. (*Throws a book.*) Right angled triangle! (*Throws a book.*) All night. Straff you all night. (*Throws a book.*) Shell and howitzer you! (*Throws a book.*) Bomb you to hell!

Throws a duster. He sits down, suddenly deflated. Smiles nervously and gets out a small cash book.

All right. All right. War's over . . . Armistice day. Demob. I suppose you want . . . compensation?

BOY. If you like, sir.

HAM. How many books did I throw?

BOY. Six, sir. Not counting the duster.

HAM. Threepence a book and say a penny the duster. Is that fair?

BOY. I'd say so, sir.

HAM. Is that one and six?

BOY. I think it's one and sevenpence, sir.

SON (*grown up*). From Ham I learnt the healing power of money ..

At one side of the stage, sitting on a bench, robed in his wig and gown and carrying his walking stick, the FATHER *is lit dictating a letter to the* MOTHER *who, wearing a hat, is sitting beside him. The* FATHER *speaks as* HAM *puts his hand in his pocket, pulls out money and counts it out and gives it to the* SON.

FATHER. I am writing to you waiting outside the President's Court to start a Divorce Case. Like all divorce cases, this one is concerned with sex, which you will find to be a subject filled with comic relief. The best part of divorce is that it is filled with comic relief . . .

JAPHET, *strumming a ukelele, appears upstage. The* BOY, *having collected his money, moves from the class towards* JAPHET. HAM *and* REIGATE *go off in different directions.*

FATHER. Pearson Dupray, K.C. who is agin me in this case is not a foeman worthy of my steel. He will no doubt fumble his cross examination and may even fail to prove my adultery . . . although God knows . . . I have had inclination and opportunity to spare.

JAPHET *starts to sing softly to his ukelele.*

JAPHET (*sings*).

> 'Hallelujah I'm a bum
> Hallelujah Bum again
> Hallelujah gives us a hand out . . .
> To revive us again . . .'

FATHER. Like you, I shall today be rubbing up against a second rate mind . . .

The SON (*as a boy*) *comes up to* JAPHET *just as* JAPHET *is starting the chorus again. The* FATHER *and* MOTHER *remain seated on their bench during the following scene.*

SON (*grown up*). Japhet, the second master, did his unsuccessful best to impart polish.

JAPHET (*sings*). 'Hallelujah . . . I'm a bum . . .'
You know what a bum is?

BOY. Yes, sir.

JAPHET (*sings*).

> 'Hallelujah. Bum again . . .
> Hallelujah, gives us a hand out . . .'

Look. No one's going to laugh if you do three simple chords. See? Three simple chords. Like this. Always. For every tune. Take my advice, and look as if you know what you're doing. No one's going to laugh. (*Looks at the* BOY.) You don't tie that tie of yours properly. Remind me to teach you to tie your tie. (*He plays a chord on the ukelele.*) Take my tip, sing in the back of your nose – so it sounds as if you'd crossed the States by railroad . . . (*He starts to sing through his nose to the ukelele.*)

JAPHET (*sings*).

> 'Why don't you go to work
> Like all the other men do?
> How the hell are we going to work
> When there's no fit work to do . . .?
> Hallelujah. I'm a bum!'

Just three simple chords. Don't get ambitious.

BOY. No, I won't, sir.

JAPHET. And remember about your tie. Twice over and then up. That way you get the big knot. Like HE wears it.

BOY. He?

JAPHET. The King, of course.

BOY. Oh yes, sir – of course.

JAPHET. The King and I – we've got a lot in common.

BOY. Yes, sir.

JAPHET. Same tie . . . same trouble.

BOY. What trouble's that, sir?

JAPHET. Woman trouble . . . Deep, deep trouble. Just like the jolly old King . . .

> JAPHET *goes sadly, carrying his ukelele. The* BOY *takes a letter out of his pocket, reads it.*

SON (*grown up*). I knew what he was talking about. He was talking about Lydia, a pale red headed girl who smelt vaguely of moth balls and who made our beds. The King and Japhet were tussling with the problems from which my father made his living.

FATHER (*dictating to the* MOTHER). You will be pleased to hear that I won Jimpson v. Jimpson, the wife being found guilty of infidelity in the front of a Daimler parked in Hampstead Garden Suburb. A vital part of the evidence consisted of footprints on the dashboard . . .

MOTHER. Is that really suitable?

FATHER (*ignoring her*). Footprints on the dashboard!

> REIGATE *comes in, bored, his hands in his pockets, and wanders near the* BOY. *The* BOY *reading the letter doesn't notice him.*

FATHER. The co-respondent was condemned in costs. My final speech lasted two hours and I made several jokes. At home we have been pricking out Korean chrysanthemums and making marmalade. Unusually large plague of earwigs this year . . .

REIGATE (*to the* BOY). Do you get many letters from home?

The FATHER *and* MOTHER *get up and the* MOTHER *leads the* FATHER *out.*

The BOY *puts the letter hurriedly back in the envelope.*

BOY. Hullo, Reigate. Once a week, I expect . . .

REIGATE. Keep the envelopes . . .

BOY. For the stamps . . .?

REIGATE. To put the fish in, on Sunday nights. The fish is disgusting. Put it in envelopes and post it down the bogs.

BOY. Why in envelopes?

REIGATE. Well you just can't put bits of fish, not straight in your pocket.

Pause.

Is your mother slim?

BOY. Fairly slim.

Pause. REIGATE *takes out a yo-yo and starts to play with it.*

REIGATE. Is your father good at golf?

BOY. Pretty good.

REIGATE (*winding up the string of his yo-yo and putting it away in his pocket*). My mother's slim as a bluebell.

BOY. Well, mine's quite slim too really. She goes to cocktail parties.

REIGATE. Slim as a bluebell! With yellow eyes.

BOY. Yellow?

REIGATE. Like a panther.

BOY. Oh, I see.

REIGATE. Very small feet. High heels of course. Does your mother wear high heels?

BOY. Whenever she goes to cocktail parties. She wears them then.

REIGATE. My mother wears high heels. *Even at breakfast.* Of course she's slim as a bluebell . . .

SON (*grown up*). But Armistice Day brought embarrasing revelaations. We were able to see those from whose loins, as Noah would say, we had actually sprung.

The BOY (*as a boy*) *and* REIGATE *part and move to opposite sides of the stage. On his side, the* BOY *is met by the* MOTHER *and the* FATHER, *come down for the Armistice Day service.* REIGATE *is met by his own* MOTHER, *a short dumpy woman in a hat and rimless spectacles, and his own* FATHER, *a nondescript grey-haired man played by* JAPHET. *Upstage a Union Jack descends. The* HEADMASTER, *to the sound of a bugle playing the Last Post, mounts an open air pulpit wearing on his gown a row of medals.*

HEADMASTER. Let us pray . . .

The parents and the boys form a congregation. MRS REIGATE *closes her eyes in an attitude of devotion. The* FATHER *blows his nose loudly.* REIGATE *stares across at him. The* BOY *looks at his* FATHER *in an agony of embarrassment, and then continues a close, and somewhat surprised study of* REIGATE'S MOTHER.

Oh Lord, inasmuch as we are paraded now on Lower School Field on this, the Armistice Day, November the Eleventh 1936, help us to remember those O.C.'s who fell upon alien soil in the late Great Match. Grant us their spirit, we beseech thee, that we may go 'over the top' to our Common Entrance and our Football Fixtures, armed with the 'cold steel' of Thy Holy Word. Give us, if Thy will be done, the Great Opportunity to shed our Blood for our Country and our Beloved School, and fill us with that feeling of Sportsmanship which led our fathers to fix bayonets and play until the last whistle blew.

THE CONGREGATION (*singing*). 'Lord God of Hosts be with us yet Lest we forget . . . Lest we forget . . .'

REIGATE'S MOTHER *is singing in a rich patriotic contralto. The* FATHER *is singing, and his mouth seems to be moving in a different time from the rest of the congregation. Gradually what he is singing becomes painfully clear over and above the reverberation of the hymn.*

FATHER (*singing*). 'She was as bee-autiful as a butterfly
And as proud as a queen
Was pretty little Polly Perkins
Of Paddington Green'.

Both the FATHER's *song and the hymn come to an end at the same time. The* HEADMASTER *has descended from his pulpit and is saying goodbye, shaking parents' hands. The parents and the* HEADMASTER *go.* REIGATE *and the* BOY *come downstage: chattering idly,* REIGATE's *hands in his pockets: the* BOY *now playing with the yo-yo.*

SON (*grown up*). Our parents, it was obvious, needed a quick coating of romance.

BOY. She didn't look much like a panther.

REIGATE. Who?

BOY. And your mother wasn't exactly a bluebell either . . .

REIGATE. My mother? You've never seen my mother . . .

BOY. Of course I have.

REIGATE. When?

BOY. On Armistice Day . . .

REIGATE. Don't be so simple. That good, honest woman isn't my *real* mother.

BOY (*puzzled*). Noah called her 'Mrs Reigate'. I heard him distinctly.

REIGATE. Noah only knows what's good for him to know. That was no more my mother than you are.

BOY. Who was she then?

REIGATE. Just the dear, good, old soul who promised to look after me.

BOY. When?

REIGATE. When they smuggled me out of Russia, after the revolution. They smuggled me out in a wickerwork trunk. I was ten days and nights on the rack in the carriage of the Siberian Railway. Then we got to Paris . . .

BOY. I thought . . .

REIGATE. They tried to shoot us in Paris. Me and my brother. But we got away, across the frozen river.

BOY. I thought Siberia was in the other direction.

REIGATE. And escaped to England. This honest chemist and his wife took care of us. Swear you won't tell anyone?

BOY. All right.

REIGATE. By the blood of my father?

BOY. If you like. I just heard from my parents actually. Something pretty sensational.

REIGATE. Oh yes?

BOY. I think they're probably . . . getting divorced.

REIGATE (*interested*). Honestly?

BOY. Honestly.

REIGATE. Why? Are they unfaithful?

BOY. Oh, always. And I told you. My mother goes to cocktail parties . . .

REIGATE (*admiringly*). You'll be having a broken home, then?

BOY (*casual*). Oh yes. I expect I will . . .

The two boys go together. Projection of the garden, trees and flowers.

SON (*grown up, to the audience*). But when I got home, nothing had changed. My home remained imperturbably intact. And, in the bracken on the common, Iris had built me a house.

Light on another part of the stage where IRIS *is kneeling, her skirt up high, her thighs scratched and stained with blackberry juice. She is arranging a handful of dead wild flowers in a chipped Coronation mug. The* SON, *as a boy, comes in. He stands beside her, aloof.*

IRIS. What do you learn at school?

BOY. We learn Latin.

IRIS. What else?

BOY. Greek.

IRIS. Say 'Good morning, what a very nice morning' in Latin.

BOY. I don't know how.

IRIS. All right. In Greek . . .

BOY. I can't.

IRIS. Why not?

BOY. They're not those sort of languages.

IRIS. What's the point of them then?

BOY. They train . . . the mind . . .

IRIS. Do you still whistle?

BOY. Not at school.

IRIS. Why not?

BOY. It's just one of those things you don't do. Like putting your hands in your pockets. You don't whistle, and you don't put your hands in your pockets.

IRIS. Why not?

BOY. You don't. That's all.

IRIS. How's your Mum and Dad?

BOY. Quarrelling.

IRIS. I never see them quarrel.

BOY. It's life . . . They come back from parties, and they quarrel.

IRIS. I shouldn't like that.

BOY. Perhaps they're not my parents, anyway . . .

IRIS. What did you say?

BOY. I said perhaps they're not my parents. Don't ask me to explain.

IRIS. I didn't.

BOY. Well – don't.

IRIS. I shan't.

BOY. It's just possible, they're not my parents. A very honest couple, but not . . .

IRIS. Of course they're your parents. Don't be ignorant.

BOY. I'm not ignorant.

IRIS. What do you know?

BOY. I know the gerund and the gerundive.

IRIS. What are they?

BOY. Something you have. In Latin. And I know the second person plural future passive of rogo.

IRIS. What is it?

BOY. Rogebamini.

IRIS. What's that mean?

BOY. It doesn't mean anything. It's just the future passive of rogo
– that's all it is . . .

    Pause.

IRIS. This is our house.

BOY (*shrugs his shoulders*). Is it?

IRIS. Shall we be Mothers and Fathers?

BOY. I think I might find that a bit painful, what with the situation
at home. Anyway, I haven't got time.

IRIS. Haven't you . . .?

BOY. Someone's coming over to see me today.

IRIS. Someone . . .?

BOY. From school. His name's Reigate actually.

IRIS. Don't you want to be Mothers and Fathers . . . (*Gets up
eagerly.*) Tell you what. I'll let you see . . . (*She pulls up her skirt
over her head, showing her knickers and a small white stomach.*)

BOY (*backing away from her*). I have to get back. Reigate's
coming to stay . . .

    Upstage a sofa. The FATHER *is sitting on it.* REIGATE *is on a
long stool holding tea and cakes. The* MOTHER *crosses to the*
FATHER *with a cup of tea, kisses him lovingly on the head and
puts the cup of tea into his hand. The* SON (*as a boy*) *moves into
the upstage area, collects a cup of tea and a bit of cake and goes
and sits by* REIGATE *on the stool.*

MOTHER. There's your tea, darling. Be careful now.

    She sits down beside the FATHER *on the sofa.*

REIGATE (*suspiciously to the* BOY). Can't see much sign of divorce
in this family.

BOY. They're putting on a show – for the visitor.

FATHER. What's going on?

MOTHER. It's the boy talking to Reigate.

FATHER. To who?

MOTHER. To Reigate . . . His friend.

FATHER (*incredulous*). The boy has a friend? (*Sudden bellow.*) Welcome, Reigate! What's Reigate like, eh? Paint me the picture . . .

MOTHER. He's quite small, and . . .

BOY. He's really Russian . . .

FATHER (*impressed*). Russian, eh? Well, that's something of an achievement . . . (*Pause.*) When I was a boy at school I never minded the lessons. I just resented having to work terribly hard at playing. (*Pause.*) They don't roast you at schools now, I suppose? I can't imagine what I'm paying all that money for if they don't roast you from time to time . . .

MOTHER. Do you like the school, Reigate?

REIGATE. It's all right. The headmaster makes us call him Noah.

SON. And his son is Shem.

REIGATE. And we have to call Mr Box and Mr Pearce Ham and Japhet. And we're the animals.

BOY. And Mr Bingo Ollard is Mr Bingo Ollard.

FATHER (*gloomily*). Didn't I warn you? Second rate minds.

REIGATE *and the* BOY *whisper to each other. Then the* BOY *gets up and goes.*

REIGATE (*to the* MOTHER). We're going to do something to keep you from thinking of your great unhappiness.

MOTHER (*giggles gently*). Our unhappiness . . . Oh . . . Whatever will they think of . . .

FATHER. What're you laughing at?

MOTHER. At Reigate!

FATHER. Who on earth's Reigate?

MOTHER. I told you, dear. The boy's friend.

FATHER. Is this Reigate then, something of a wit?

MOTHER. He does come out with some killing suggestions.

REIGATE (*dignified*). We're going to do a play.

FATHER. What's that?

MOTHER. They're going to put on an entertainment.

> *The* BOY *comes in, dragging an old dressing-up box from which he pulls an old tin hat, a khaki cap, a khaki jacket, a Sam Browne belt, a revolver holster, a water bottle and a bayonet: the* FATHER'S *uniform equipment from the 1914 war which he and* REIGATE *proceed to share between them.*

FATHER. I like entertainment. When's it to be?

BOY. This afternoon.

MOTHER. Better hurry. Mr Lean's coming to drive you back to school at four.

FATHER. What is it? Something out of the *Boys' Own*?

BOY. I wrote it.

FATHER. What?

MOTHER. The boy said he wrote it. I'm sure Reigate helped. Didn't you, Reigate?

BOY. He didn't help.

MOTHER. Whatever are you? Two little clowns?

REIGATE. Actually we're two subalterns. Killed on the Somme.

FATHER. Hm. They'll soon be giving us war again. When it comes, remember this. Avoid the temptation to do anything heroic.

> REIGATE *goes out of the room, wearing a tin hat and a khaki jacket and the bayonet. The* BOY *is wearing the khaki cap and the Sam Browne.*

Tell me what's going on. Make it vivid.

MOTHER. They've got your barbed wire.

> REIGATE *returns pulling a roll of barbed wire which he leaves in the middle of the floor.*

FATHER. My what?

MOTHER. Barbed wire.

FATHER. Put it back, won't you? We don't want the cows in.

MOTHER. Reigate's got your tin hat. And the boy's wearing your old Sam Browne.

FATHER. How killing!

> REIGATE *and the* BOY *take green flashlights from the dressing-up box, turn out the lights in the room and approach each other shining green lights in each other's faces and moaning in a ghostly fashion.*

MOTHER. We can see Reigate's artistic! He's giving a lively performance . . .

REIGATE. Actually we're ghosts.

FATHER. Ghosts eh? What're they doing now.

BOY. We're meeting after the bombardment.

MOTHER. They're meeting after the bombardment, dear.

FATHER. How very killing!

BOY. Bill . . .

REIGATE. Who is it . . .?

BOY. It's me, Bill . . . It's Harry.

REIGATE. Harry! I can't see you, old fellow. (*Coughs.*) It's this damn gas everywhere. Take my hand.

BOY. Where are you?

REIGATE. Out here – by the wire. Listen.

BOY. What?

REIGATE. They've stopped straffing. I say, if ever we get back to the old country –

BOY. What?

REIGATE. I want you to marry Helen.

BOY. You said you'd never let Helen marry a chap who'd funked the top board at Roehampton . . .

REIGATE. Never mind what I said, Harry. I saw you today on the North redoubt; you were in there, batting for England! You shall have my little sister, boy. My hand on it.

BOY. I can't feel your hand, Bill.

REIGATE. I can't see you, Harry.

BOY. I'm cold . . .

REIGATE. I'm afraid we'll never see England again.

BOY. What's the matter with us, Bill?

REIGATE (*beginning to laugh*). We're dead, old fellow. Can't you understand? We're both of us – dead!

They are both overcome with laughter and collapse in hoots and giggles. Their green flashlights go out; and the light is concentrated on the FATHER *on the sofa while the* MOTHER *supervises the two boys clearing away the barbed wire, dressing-up box etc. During the following speech, they all go off with these things, leaving the* FATHER *alone on the stage.*

FATHER (*laughing*). Dead . . . how killing! (*Serious.*) You know. I didn't want to be dead. I never wanted that. When I got married – at Saffron Walden, they were just about to pack me off to France. Bands. Troop ships. Flowers thrown at you . . . and dead in a fortnight. I didn't want anything to do with it . . . And then, the day before we were due to go my old Major drew me aside and he said 'You've just got married old fellow. No particular sense in being dead!' He'd found me a post in the Inland Waterways! That's my advice to you, if they look like giving us war. Get yourself a job in the Inland Waterways . . .

The light fades on the FATHER *upstage and is concentrated on* REIGATE *and the* BOY *as they enter upstage in school uniform, walking side by side. As they start to speak, the* FATHER *gets up, tapping his way with his stick, leaves the stage.*

REIGATE. Your parents seem to be getting on quite well.
BOY. They pretend – for me.
REIGATE. Your mother didn't seem to drink very much either.
BOY. Not till the evenings.

Light increases upstage where JAPHET *enters with a portable gramophone which he puts down on a table and puts on a record.*

REIGATE. That was good advice your father gave us – about the Inland Waterways . . .
BOY. Yes.
REIGATE. You know? I'll tell you something about your father . . .

BOY. What?

REIGATE. He can't see ... He's blind, isn't he?

SON (*grown up, to the audience*). It was a question our family never asked. Naturally I didn't answer it.

Pause. The SON (*as a boy*) *says nothing.* JAPHET's *record starts to play 'Smoke gets in your eyes'. The* BOY *turns sharply away from* REIGATE *and moves towards* JAPHET. JAPHET *holds up his arms and he and the* BOY *silently start to dance together to 'Smoke gets in your eyes'.* REIGATE *looks after the son, shrugs his shoulders then crosses the stage and goes.*

JAPHET. Slow, quick, slow. Slow, quick, slow. Chassis! No – chassis! Look! (*They dance a few more bars together, awkwardly, at arm's length.*) How're you going to get through life if you can't do the slow foxtrot ...? That's the trouble with education. It never teaches you anything worth knowing. Half the boys here've got no idea of tying their ties, let alone tango ... Sorry you're leaving ...?

BOY. Not altogether ...

The music stops. JAPHET *takes off the record, studies it, embarrassed.*

JAPHET. I'm leaving too. Perhaps you heard ...?

BOY. Yes, sir, I know. Lydia left yesterday. We had to make our own beds this morning.

JAPHET. Lydia's left. I've resigned. So has the poor old King.

BOY. Him as well ...?

JAPHET. He broadcast this afternoon. We heard it on Noah's radiogram. The King has given up everything for love. I told you we had a lot in common ...

Pause.

Take my advice. Don't give up everything for love ...

BOY. No, sir.

JAPHET. It's just not on – that's all. Just simply not on ...

BOY. You coming to Noah's talk, sir? It's for all of us leavers.

JAPHET. The one where he tells you the facts of life . . .?

BOY. I think that's the one.

JAPHET. No. I shall stay away. I've heard quite enough about *them* to be going on with . . .

> The HEADMASTER *appears downstage, wearing a tweed jacket with leather patches and smoking a pipe.* REIGATE *comes in and sits on the floor gazing up at him respectfully.* JAPHET, *upstage, packs up his gramophone and goes. The* BOY *moves upstage.*

HEADMASTER. You are the leavers! In a month or two you will go on to Great Public Schools, away from this warm cosy little establishment. (*The* BOY *arrives and stands and knocks.*) Come in. You're disturbing everybody. Shut the door, boy. Most terrible draught. (*The* BOY *moves in and sits down next to* REIGATE.) Ah now . . . Before I forget, Mrs Noah and I will be pleased to see you all to tea on Sunday. A trifling matter of anchovy paste sandwiches! Do you hear that, eh Reigate? All come with clean finger nails, no boy to put butter on his hair.

REIGATE. Please, sir?

HEADMASTER. Yes, Reigate.

REIGATE. Why aren't we to put butter on our hair?

HEADMASTER. Ah! Good question. I'm glad you asked me that! We had that trouble with the native regiments. They licked down their hair with butter. It went rancid in the hot weather. Unpleasant odour on parade. There's no law against a drop of water on the comb. Now . . . What was I going to tell you? Ah! I was warning you about dreams. You'll have them. Oh, certainly you'll have them. And in the morning you may feel like saying to yourselves, 'You rotter! To have a dream like that!' Well, you can't help it. That's all. You simply can't help them. Not dreams. If you're awake of course, you can do something about it. You can change into a pair of shorts and go for a run across country. Or you can get into a bath, and turn on the cold tap. You can quite easily do that. Your housemaster will understand. He'll understand if you should've been up to a French lesson, or Matins or some such thing. Simply say, Sir, I had to have a bath, or a run, or whatever it is. Just say to Mr Raffles, or Humphrey Stiggler, or Percy Parr, just say, Mr Parr, or Mr Raffles, dependant on which school you're at of course, this is what I felt the need to do. He'll understand perfectly. Another thing! Simply this. When sleeping always lie on the right side. Not on the face, for obvious reasons. Not on the back. Brings on dreams. Not on the left side. Stops the heart. Just the right side . . . all the time. Now then, to the most serious problems you're likely to run up against. Friends. You may find that some boy from another class, or a house even, comes up to you and says 'Let's be friends' or even offers you a slice of cake. That's a very simple one, a perfectly simple one to deal with. Just say loudly 'I'm going straight to tell the housemaster'. Straight away. No hesitation about it. Remember, the only real drawback to our Great Public School system is unsolicited cake – Have you got that very clear? Go straight and tell the Housemaster.

    BOY *and* REIGATE *get up, stretch, and wander off.* REIGATE *playing with the yo-yo which he gets out of his pocket.*

REIGATE. Do you have dreams?

BOY. Not very much . . .

REIGATE. I once dreamt about fish.

BOY. What?

REIGATE. All that fish. You know the fish we had on Sunday nights. That we put down the loo. I dreamt it came swimming back at us. I dreamt it all swam back in shoals, and invaded the school.

BOY. Did you feel bad? About dreaming that, I mean.

REIGATE. I suppose so.

BOY. That must've been what he meant.

    They go. Upstage lit, the FATHER *and* MOTHER *are sitting on two garden chairs, beside a tea trolley. An empty chair beside them. Downstage the* SON (*grown up*) *speaks to the audience, he is putting on a school blazer and knitting a silk scarf round his neck.*

SON (*grown up*). It wasn't until later that I realized the headmaster had been trying to advise us on a subject my father often brought up unexpectedly, in the middle of tea.

The SON (*as a boy*) *enters upstage, sits in the empty chair beside his* FATHER *and* MOTHER, *takes a biscuit, lounges, chewing it as the* MOTHER *pours tea. Pause, before the* FATHER *speaks.*

FATHER. Sex! It's been greatly over-rated by the poets . . .

MOTHER. Would you like your biscuit now, dear? (*She puts a biscuit beside him on a plate.*)

FATHER. I never had many mistresses with thighs like white marble. Is the tea pot exhausted?

MOTHER. I'm putting some more hot water in now.

The MOTHER *continues pouring tea. The meal goes on.*

SON (*grown up, to the audience*). What did he mean? That he'd had many mistresses without especially marmoreal thighs – or few mistresses of any sort?

FATHER (*suddenly*). 'Change in a trice
The lilies and languors of virtue
For the roses and raptures of vice!'
Where's my bloody biscuit . . .?

MOTHER. I put it beside you, dear.

FATHER. 'From their lips have thy lips taken fever?
Is the breath of them hot in thy hair . . .?'

SON (*grown up, to the audience*). What did he know of the sharp uncertainties of love?

The SON (*grown up*) *turns and moves upstage. He taps the* BOY *on the shoulder and motions him to move. The* BOY *gets up reluctantly and leaves the stage, chewing his biscuit. The* SON (*grown up*) *takes his chair and sits, the* MOTHER *hands him a cup of tea.*

FATHER (*suddenly laughing*). 'Is the breath of them hot in thy
hair?' How perfectly revolting it sounds! Sex is pretty uphill
work, if you want my opinion.

SON. I don't agree.

FATHER. What?

SON. I don't happen to agree.

FATHER. Who's that?

MOTHER. It's the boy. (*She looks at him, gives a small laugh.*)
Whatever have you got on?

FATHER. The boy's been very quiet lately.

MOTHER. He's wearing my old scarf from Liberties. Tied as a
cravat.

FATHER. A cravat eh? How killing! (*Pause.*) Is that what it is? Do
you have your own thoughts?

SON. I don't think sex has been overrated exactly.

FATHER. I'll tell you a story. A lover, a wife and an angry husband . . .

MOTHER (*calm*). Not that one, dear. (*To the* SON.) You'll have
some tea?

FATHER. Whyever not?

MOTHER. It's not very suitable. (*To the* SON, *vaguely*) Do you like
sugar? I always forget.

SON. No thanks.

FATHER. The husband returns and discovers all! He summons the
lover into the dining room. The wife waits, trembling, terrified,
for the sounds of fighting, the smashing of crockery. Silence.
She tiptoes down the stairs. There's the husband and the lover
side by side at the table, perfectly contented, drinking light ale.
Suddenly she bursts out at both of them – 'You ungrateful
brutes!' They both listen as the door slams after her. They open
another bottle of light ale. 'Ungrateful brutes!' That was the
expression she used!

Pause. The SON *looks at him.*

SON. Did that really happen?

FATHER. What?

SON. Did that ever really happen?

Pause.

FATHER. Sex! The whole business has been over-estimated by the poets.

The SON *looks at his watch, gets up, kisses his* MOTHER *and moves downstage. He takes a cigarette case out of his inside blazer pocket and lights a cigarette with careless expertise. He moves to a downstage corner where, separately and pinkly lit, two women enter smoking through holders. They are* MISS COX, *small and fluffy, nursing a poodle, and* MISS BAKER, *in trousers and a beret. Furniture set in their area includes a drawing by Cocteau of a sailor, and a white macaw in a cage. Somewhere a portable radio is softly playing 'La Vie en Rose' as* MISS BAKER *hands pink drinks to* MISS COX *and the* SON.

Upstage the FATHER *and the* MOTHER *continue to talk.*

FATHER. Where's the boy?

MOTHER. Gone out. He's paying a call.

FATHER (*incredulous*). Gone out – as a visitor?

MOTHER. Yes. To tea. With Miss Baker and Miss Cox.

FATHER. Who are they?

MOTHER. They run the new book shop. By the station. Apparently he went in to buy a book and they asked him round to tea – as a visitor. I expect that's the notion behind his extraordinary cravat.

FATHER. Not bringing them back here, is he?

MOTHER. He didn't say so.

FATHER. If he does, I shall lie doggo! I shall go to earth, in the West Copse. I shall hide myself . . . I promise you . . .

MOTHER. No, he didn't say he was bringing them back here . . .

FATHER. Well, I shall disappear without a trace if he does.

He feels for his stick, struggles to his feet. The MOTHER *stands up and takes his arm.*

Doesn't he know? We dread visitors. (*Pause.*) Poor boy, to have to go out. He'll miss the evening foray after earwigs.

The MOTHER *and the* FATHER *walk off together.*

MISS COX. I could've kissed you when you came in to our shop.

SON. Could you really?

MISS BAKER. And actually bought a book!

MISS COX. Most people come in for pamphlets. A hundred things to do with dried egg – published by the Ministry of Food . . .

The radio stops playing 'La Vie en Rose'. A BBC ANNOUNCER *speaks cheerily.*

ANNOUNCER'S VOICE. 'What do I do if I come across German or Italian broadcasts when tuning my wireless? I say to myself: "Now this blighter wants me to listen to him. Am I going to do what this blighter wants?"'

MISS BAKER (*switches the radio off*). We'll have to give up that shop.

SON. Why will you?

MISS COX. Bill's going to be called up.

SON. Who's Bill?

MISS BAKER I'm Bill. (*She picks up a bit of bread and butter and waves it at* MISS COX.) She's Daphne . . . (*She goes to the macaw's cage, prods a piece of bread and butter through the cage bars.*) . . . This bloody bird gets half my butter ration . . .

MISS COX. They're putting Bill on the land . . .

MISS BAKER. I'll probably ruin the crops.

MISS COX. I'll send you off in the morning darling . . . with a meat pie and a little bottle of cold tea.

MISS BAKER. Thank you very much!

MISS COX. It's the war, Bill! We all have to make sacrifices. (*To* SON.) Bill doesn't much care for this war. We were more keen on the war in Spain.

MISS BAKER. And in the evenings, I suppose you'll wash me down in front of the fire. (*To the macaw.*) Eat up, Miss Garbo!

MISS COX. Nonsense. They're not sending you down the mines!
(*To the* SON.) All our friends were awfully keen on the war in
Spain; Stephen Spender and all that jolly collection . . . I expect
you'll go into the Fire Service . . .?

SON. Why?

MISS COX. All our friends go into the Fire Service.

MISS BAKER. They get a lot of time for writing, waiting about
between fires . . .

SON. My father says I should avoid the temptation to do anything
heroic . . .

Change of light, projection of a darker garden upstage. The
MOTHER *comes in, leading the* FATHER, *carrying his camp stool*
and a bucket. She sits him down in front of a plant with inverted
flower pots on a stick around it. Then she leaves him. He begins
to feel for the pots and empty them in the bucket.

MISS COX. We've never actually met your father . . .

MISS BAKER. We looked over the gate one evening and shouted –
but he was busy in the garden doing something.

SON. Probably the earwigs.

MISS BAKER. What?

SON. He drowns the earwigs every night.

MISS COX. How most extraordinary . . .

She gets up and starts putting things back on the tea tray.

The Fire Service! That's where you'll end up. It gives everyone
far more time to write.

MISS BAKER. Is that what you're going to be then – a writer?

Pause. Change of light. The light fades on MISS COX *and*
MISS BAKER'S *part of the stage, and increases on the* FATHER
as the SON *leaves the two ladies, and walks across to join the*
FATHER. *On his way he collects a camp stool and puts it up and*
sits beside the FATHER. *He starts to help him with the earwig*
traps, taking off the inverted flower pots and emptying the ear-

wigs that have gone in there for warmth and shelter, into the bucket of water to drown miserably. MISS BAKER *and* MISS COX *go.*

FATHER. Is that you?

SON. Yes, it's me.

FATHER. What're you doing?

SON. Helping you.

FATHER. Consider the persistence of the earwig! Each afternoon, it feasts on the dahlia blooms. Each night it crawls into our flower pots to sleep. Each morning, we empty the flower pots and drown the earwig ... but still they come! Nature's remorseless.

SON. I may be a writer ...

FATHER. If we did this for one million years all over the world, could we make some small dent in the pattern of evolution? Would we produce an earwig that could swim? (*Pause.*) You'd be better off in the law ...

SON. I'd like to write ...

FATHER. You'll have plenty of spare time! My first five years in Chambers, I did nothing but *The Times* crossword puzzle. Besides which, if you were only a writer, who would you rub shoulders with? (*With contempt.*) Other writers? You'll be far better off in the law.

SON. I don't know ...

FATHER. No brilliance is needed in the law. Nothing but common sense, and relatively clean finger nails. Another thing, if you were a writer, think of your poor, unfortunate wife ...

SON. What?

FATHER. She'd have you at home every day! In carpet slippers ... Drinking tea and stumped for words! You'd be far better off down the tube each morning, and off to the Law Courts ... How many have we bagged today?

SON (*looking down into the bucket*). About a hundred.

FATHER. A moderate bag, I'd say. Merely moderate. You know,

the law of husband and wife might seem idiotic at first sight. But when you get to know it, you'll find it can exercise a vague medieval charm. Learn a little law, won't you? Just to please me . . .

The MOTHER *enters. She goes up to the* FATHER, *touches him.*

MOTHER. Your bath's ready.

FATHER. What?

MOTHER. I said your bath water's nice and hot.

He gets up, takes her arm. She starts to lead him off the stage.

I suppose there isn't an easier way of getting rid of earwigs?

FATHER. An easier way! Sometimes I wonder if women understand anything.

They go. The SON *stands, then moves down towards the audience. The light changes and the garden fades on the back-cloth, to be replaced by a pattern of Gothic arches. The* SON *speaks to the audience, downstage right.*

SON. It was my father's way to offer the law to me – the great stone column of authority which has been dragged by an adulterous, careless, negligent and half criminal humanity down the ages – as if it were a small mechanical toy which might occupy half an hour on a rainy afternoon.

Upstage a Judge's chair with a coat of arms, a witness box. A JUDGE *enters, and takes his place : from offstage left, the sound of footsteps on a stone passage and the tapping of a stick. Then the* FATHER *and* MOTHER *enter downstage left. The* FATHER *is now wearing a black jacket and a winged collar and bow tie. The* MOTHER *stations the* FATHER *by one of the cubes on which a mirror is hanging. She goes out and returns with his wig, gown and white bands to take the place of his tie, and helps him to change. The opposing barrister,* MR BOUSTEAD, *robed, but carrying his wig, comes and starts to comb his hair in front of the mirror.*

SON (*to the audience*). He never used a white stick – but his clouded malacca was heard daily, tapping the cold stone corridors of the Law Courts. He had no use for dogs, therapy, training, nor did he adapt himself to his condition. He simply pretended that nothing had happened. (*The* SON *goes.*)

BOUSTEAD. Good morning.

FATHER. Who's that?

MOTHER. It's Mr Boustead, dear . . . He's for the husband.

FATHER. Agin me, Bulstrode. Are you agin me?

BOUSTEAD. Boustead.

FATHER. Excuse me. Boustead of course. Where are you?

BOUSTEAD. Here, I'm here . . .

FATHER. I have studied your case pretty closely and I have a suggestion to make which you might find helpful.

BOUSTEAD. Really?

FATHER. What I was suggesting, entirely for your assistance of course – is that you might like – my dear boy – to throw in your hand . . . Now, is that a help to you . . . ?

BOUSTEAD. Certainly not! I'd say we have some pretty valuable evidence . . .

Light change. In the witness box appears MR THONG, *a private detective of a crafty appearance, wearing a brown suit and a cycling club badge on his lapel.* BOUSTEAD *moves to upstage right, stands questioning him. The* MOTHER *leads the* FATHER *to his seat left and sits behind him.*

BOUSTEAD. Now from the vantage point which you have described, Mr Thong, will you tell my Lord and the Jury exactly what you saw?

The FATHER *turns and speaks in a loud stage whisper to the* MOTHER.

FATHER. Throat spray!

The MOTHER *puts a small throat spray into the* FATHER'S *hand.* THONG *consults his notebook.*

BOUSTEAD. Yes, Mr Thong, in your own words.

FATHER (*loud whisper*). Thanks.

THONG (*monotonously, reading his notebook*). From my point of vantage, I was quite clearly able to see inside the kitchen window . . .

BOUSTEAD. Yes?

THONG. And –

> The FATHER *opens his mouth and starts, very loudly, to spray his throat.*

JUDGE. Speak up, Mr Thong, I can't hear you.

THONG. My Lord. I was able to distinguish clearly the Respondent . . .

JUDGE (*writing carefully*). Yes. . .

THONG. In the act of . . . (*His mumble is again drowned by the* FATHER's *work with the throat spray.*) . . . with a man distinguishable only by a small moustache . . . I now recognize him as the Co-Respondent, Dacres.

BOUSTEAD. In the act of what, Mr Thong?

THONG. The act of . . . (*The* FATHER *works the throat spray very loudly.*

BOUSTEAD. If my learned friend would allow us to hear the evidence . . .

FATHER (*puts down the throat spray and whispers deafeningly to* BOUSTEAD). I'm so sorry. My dear boy, if *this* is the valuable evidence you told me about, I shall be quiet – as the tomb . . .!

BOUSTEAD (*firmly*). Mr Thong.

FATHER (*half rising to address the* JUDGE). By all means, my Lord. Let us hear this *valuable* evidence.

JUDGE. Very well.

THONG. I distinctly saw them . . .

JUDGE. Distinctly saw them what?

THONG. Kissing and cuddling, my Lord.

BOUSTEAD. And then . . .

THONG. The light was extinguished . . .

BOUSTEAD. Where?

THONG. In the kitchen.

BOUSTEAD. And a further light appeared?

THONG. In the bedroom.

JUDGE. For a moment?

THONG. Merely momentarily, my Lord.

BOUSTEAD. So . . .

THONG. The house was shrouded in darkness. And the Co-Respondent, this is the point that struck us, had not emerged.

BOUSTEAD. And you kept up observation until . . .

THONG. Approximately, dawn.

BOUSTEAD (*very satisfied, as he sits down*). Thank you, Mr Thong.

The FATHER *rises, clattering. Folds his hands on his stomach, gazes sightlessly at* MR THONG *and then allows a long pause during which* MR THONG *stirs uncomfortably. Then he starts quietly, slowly working himself up into a climax.*

FATHER. Mr Thong, what price did you put on this valuable evidence?

THONG. I don't know what you mean . . .

FATHER. You have been paid, haven't you, to give it?

THONG. I'm a private enquiry agent . . .

FATHER. A professional witness?

THONG. Charging the usual fee.

FATHER. Thirty pieces of silver?

BOUSTEAD (*rises, indignant*). My Lord, I object. This is outrageous.

JUDGE. Perhaps that was not entirely relevant. (BOUSTEAD *subsides.*)

FATHER. Then let me ask you something which is very relevant. Which goes straight to the secret heart of this wretched little conspiracy. Where was this lady's husband during your observations?

THONG. Captain Waring?

FATHER. Yes. Captain Waring.

THONG. He had accompanied me . . .

FATHER. Why?

THONG. For the purpose of . . .

FATHER. For the purpose of what . . .?

THONG. Identification . . .

FATHER. And how long did he remain with you?

THONG. As long as observation continued . . .

FATHER. Till dawn . . .?

THONG. Until approximately 5.30 a.m.

FATHER. And did he not storm the house? Did he not beat upon the door? Did he not seize his wife's paramour by the throat and hurl him into the gutter?

THONG. According to my notebook. No.

FATHER. And according to your notebook, was he enjoying himself?

BOUSTEAD (*driven beyond endurance, rises to protest*). Really . . .!

FATHER. Please, Mr Bulstrode! I've sat here for three days! Like patience on a monument! Whilst a series of spiteful, mean, petty, trumped-up sickening and small-minded charges are tediously paraded against the unfortunate woman I represent. And now, when I rise to cross-examine . . . *I will not be interrupted!*

JUDGE. Gentlemen! Please, gentlemen. (*To* FATHER.) What was your question?

FATHER. I've forgotten it. My learned friend's interruption has had the effect he no doubt intended and I have forgotten my question!

BOUSTEAD. This is quite intolerable . . .

FATHER. Ah . . . Now I've remembered it again. Did he enjoy the night, Thong, in this field . . . from which he was magically able to overlook his own kitchen . . .?

THONG. This plot of waste ground . . .

FATHER. Up a tree, was he?

THONG. What?

FATHER. Was he perched upon a tree?

THONG. We had stepped up, into the lower branches.

FATHER. Was it the naked eye?

THONG. Pardon?

FATHER. Was he viewing this distressing scene by aid of the naked eye?

THONG. Captain Waring had brought a pair of field glasses.

FATHER. His racing glasses . . .?

THONG. I . . .

JUDGE. Speak up, Mr Thong.

THONG. I imagine he used them for racing, my Lord.

FATHER. You see Captain Waring has given evidence in this Court.

BOUSTEAD (*ironic*). On the subject of his racing glasses?

FATHER (*his voice filled with passion*). No, Mr Bulstrode. On the subject of love. He has told us that he was deeply, sincerely in love with his wife.

THONG. I don't know anything about that.

FATHER. Exactly, Mr Thong! You are hardly an expert witness, are you, on the subject of love?

Light change. MR THONG *leaves the witness box.* BOUSTEAD *leaves also. The* FATHER *is standing as if addressing the Jury.*

May it please you, my Lord, Members of the Jury. Love has driven men and women in the course of history to curious extremes. Love tempted Leander to plunge in and swim the raging Hellespont. It led Juliet to feign death and Ophelia to madness. No doubt it complicated the serenity of the Garden of Eden and started the Trojan War: but surely there is no more curious example of the mysterious effects of the passion than the spectacle of Captain Waring of the Royal Engineers, roosted in a tree, complacently viewing the seduction of his beloved through a pair of strong racing binoculars . . .

The light fades altogether on the back of the upstage areas. The FATHER's *voice comes out of the shadows.*

Is not the whole story, Members of the Jury, an improbable and impertinent tissue of falsehood . . .?

The SON *is lit downstage as in the upstage darkness, the* JUDGE, *the* FATHER, *and the* MOTHER *go and the Courtroom furniture is moved away.*

SON (*to the audience*). He sent words out into the darkness, like soldiers sent off to battle, and was never short of reinforcements. In the Law Courts he gave his public performance. At home he returned to his private ritual, the potting shed, the crossword puzzle and, when I was at home, the afternoon walk.

Projection of trees as the upstage area becomes slowly lighter.

The woods were dark and full of flies. We picked bracken leaves to swat them, and when I was a child he told me we carried cutlasses to hack our way through the jungle. I used to shut my eyes at dead rats, or magpies gibbeted on the trees: sights his blindness spared him. He walked with his hand on my arm. A small hand, with loose brown skin. From time to time, I had an urge to pull away from him, to run into the trees and hide . . . to leave him alone, lost in perpetual darkness. But then his hand would tighten on my sleeve; he was very persistent . . .

The SON *walks behind a cube and emerges with the* FATHER *who is wearing a tweed jacket and his straw hat and is holding the* SON's *arm tightly as they walk round the stage, slowly towards a raised platform upstage . . .*

FATHER. I've had a good deal of fun . . . out of the law.

SON. Have you ever been to the South of France?

FATHER. Once or twice. It's all right, except for the dreadful greasy food they can't stop talking about.

SON. Bill and Daphne say the worst of the War is that they can't get to the South of France.

FATHER. Who're they?

SON. Two ladies from the book shop.

FATHER. Where you had to go, as a visitor?

SON. That's right.

FATHER. My heart bled for you on that occasion.

SON. Daphne's Miss Cox.

FATHER. And Bill . . .?

SON. . . . Bill's Miss Baker.

FATHER. Damned rum!

SON. Before the War they practically lived in Cannes. They met Cocteau . . .

FATHER. Who?

SON. He smoked opium. Have you ever smoked opium?

FATHER. Certainly not! Gives you constipation. Dreadful binding effect. Ever seen those pictures of the wretched poet Coleridge? Green around the gills. And a stranger to the lavatory. Avoid opium.

SON. They may find me a war job.

FATHER. Who?

SON. Miss Baker and Miss Cox.

FATHER. Why, is 'Bill' on the General Staff?

SON. They have a friend who makes propaganda films for the government. He needs an assistant.

FATHER. You're thinking of entering the film world?

SON. Just . . . for the duration.

FATHER. Well! At least there's nothing heroic about it.

SON. No.

FATHER. Rum sort of world, isn't it – the film world?

SON. I expect so.

FATHER. Don't they wear their caps *back to front* in the film world?

SON. You're thinking of the silent days.

FATHER. Am I? Perhaps I am. Your mother and I went to a silent film once. In Glastonbury.

SON. Did you?

FATHER. We were staying there in an hotel. Damn dull. Nothing to do in the evenings. So we sallied forth, to see this silent film.

The point was, I invariably dressed for dinner, when in Glastonbury. Follow?

SON. I follow.

FATHER. And when your mother and I entered this picture palace – in evening dress – the whole audience burst into spontaneous applause! I believe they took us for part of the entertainment! ... Rum kind of world I must say. Where are we?

SON. At the bottom of Stonor hill.

FATHER. I'll rest for a moment. Then we'll go up to the top.

The SON *moves him to the right of the platform and sits him down.*

SON. Will we?

FATHER. Of course we will! You can see the three counties from the top of Stonor Hill. Don't you want to see three counties ...?

SON. All right.

FATHER. See everything. Everything in Nature ... That's the instinct of the May beetle. Twenty-four hours to live, so spend it ... looking around.

SON. We've got more time ...

FATHER. Don't you believe it! It's short ... but enjoyable! You know what? If they ever say to you – 'your old Father, he couldn't have enjoyed life much. Overdrawn at the Bank and bad-tempered and people didn't often visit him ...' 'Nonsense' you can say. 'He enjoyed every minute of it ...'

SON. Do you want to go on now?

FATHER. When you consider the embryo of the liver fluke, born in sheeps' droppings, searching the world for a shell to bore into for the sake of living in a snail until it becomes tadpole-like and leaves its host – and then gets swallowed up by a sheep again! When you consider that – complicated persistence, well, of course, I've clung on for sixty five years. It's the instinct – that's all. The irresistible instinct! All right. We'll go up ... Watch carefully and you'll see three counties ...

He puts out his hand, the SON *pulls him up. They walk off behind a cube. Light change. The projection of trees changes to blue sky*

and small clouds. On the platform, MISS COX *and* MISS
BAKER *are sunbathing: wearing bathing suits, lying on a rug,
their arms around each other. They are kissing as the* FATHER
and SON *re-appear breathless after their climb. The* SON *says
nothing.* MISS BAKER *puts a hand over* MISS COX's *mouth.*

What can you see?

SON. Three counties ...

FATHER. Be my eyes then. Paint me the picture ...

SON (*pause*). We can just see three counties. Stretched out. That's
all we can see.

FATHER. A fine prospect?

SON. Yes. A fine prospect.

FATHER. We've bagged a good many sights today! What've we
seen?

SON. We saw a hare. Oh, and that butterfly.

FATHER. Danaius Chrysippus! The one that flaunts a large type
of powder puff. You described it to me. You painted me the
picture.

SON. Shall we go home now?

FATHER. We saw a lot today.

As the SON *moves back towards the door the* FATHER *moves
with him.*

We saw a good deal – of the monstrous persistence of Nature ...

The FATHER *and the* SON *move away.* MISS BAKER *takes her
hand off* MISS COX's *mouth releasing a cascade of giggles as the
light fades.*

ACT TWO

Light downstage. Noise of carpentry, shouting, singing and cursing. A movie camera on a tripod is set somewhere downstage. Film technicians, a SPARKS trundling a 2K and a CHIPPY with a trestle and a bit of wood, enter. The CHIPPY starts to saw noisily. The DIRECTOR, wearing a sheepskin flying jacket, fur boots and a woollen hat, comes in smoking a Wills Whiff and looks into the camera. The stage management of the play should come on the stage in this scene and become the film technicians, cameramen etc. Projection on the backcloth suggests a cloudy sky, a radar installation and observation post 'somewhere in England during the War'.

SPARKS (*singing loudly*).
> 'Oh Salome, Salome
> That's my girl, Salome.
> Standing there with her arse all bare . . .'

The SON enters. He is carrying a glossy magazine called Kinema Arts *and wearing dark glasses. He looks round, lost.* DORIS *enters. She's the Unit Manager. A tough, very competent, deep voiced woman also wearing a sheepskin flying jacket, flying boots and a G.I.'s cap on her orange hair. She also has a cigarette drooping from pillarbox red lips, and is carrying a clip board with the script, schedule etc. on it. She approaches the SON with a military swagger.*

DORIS (*yells*). Let's have some quiet please! (*The noise stops. To* SON.) You the new assistant . . .?

SON (*nervous*). Yes?

SPARKS (*singing quietly*).
> 'Every little wrinkle made the boys all stare . . .'

DORIS (*full throated roar*). Great Scott, Sparks! I can't hear this boy.

SPARKS. Sorry, Doris.

He stops singing.

DORIS. Know your job, do you . . .?

SON. I'm new to movies . . .

DORIS. Great Scott! You don't have to know anything about movies. You're here to fetch the subsistence . . .

SON. The what?

DORIS. Tea breaks. Coffee breaks. After lunch special refreshment and in lieu of breakfast breaks. The Sparks have tea and ham and lettuce rolls, known to them as smiggett sandwiches. The Chippies take coffee and cakes with coconut icing. The director needs Horlicks, liver pâté sandwiches and Wills Whiffs. Keep your mouth shut except to call in a firm and authoritative manner for 'Quiet' when we shoot. Any questions?

SON. Yes.

DORIS. What?

SON. Where do I get liver pâté sandwiches?

DORIS. Use your bloody imagination! That's what you came into the film business for . . .

DIRECTOR (*calling her from the camera*). Doris!

DORIS. Coming, Humphrey. (*To the* SON.) Remember, next tea break in ten minutes. (*She goes to chatter to the* DIRECTOR.)

SPARKS *comes up to the puzzled looking* SON. *Talks at great speed.*

SPARKS. You looking for something?

SON. Well, yes.

SPARKS. Don't worry. Maybe you left it in the Officers' Mess. You know we've got two ATS in the next scene?

SON. I didn't know.

SPARKS. There's two sorts of ATS let me tell you. Cocked ATS and felt ATS. Had it in last night, did you?

SON. What did you say?

SPARKS. Seen the King last night?

SON. No. (*Innocent.*) Was he here?

SPARKS. Was he here! . . . That's a good one. Who did you say
   you was out with?

> *Upstage two ATS girls apppear in uniform. One scans the sky
> with binoculars. The other starts to pour tea. The camera is
> focused on them. A STAGE MANAGER holds a microphone on the
> end of a long bamboo pole near to them.*

SON. Actually . . . No one.

SPARKS. Didn't spend out on her, I hope? Never spend out till
   you get lucky . . . Then you can buy her a packet of small
   smokes.

DIRECTOR. All right, we'll try a rehearsal.

SPARKS. What did you say you was looking for?

SON. A liver pâté sandwich.

SPARKS. A liver pâté . . . You're a caution! That's what you are.

DORIS. Rehearsal!

> *The ATS GIRLS start to speak. SPARKS returns to his light
> which is switched on them. The SON wanders off disconsolately.
> Other members of the Unit start a game of pontoon somewhere.*

FIRST ATS GIRL. Gerry a bit naughty tonight, Hilda.

SECOND ATS GIRL. Yes. (*She offers the other a mug of tea.*) Tea,
   luv?

FIRST ATS GIRL (*lowers her binoculars*). Ta, luv.

SECOND ATS GIRL. Sugars, do you?

FIRST ATS GIRL. Ta.

SECOND ATS GIRL. One or two sugars?

FIRST ATS GIRL. Two, ta. (*Pause*). Ta.

> *Pause.*

SECOND ATS GIRL. You know, I've been thinking lately.

FIRST ATS GIRL. Have you, luv?

The SON *comes back with a tray, starts handing tea and sandwiches round the Unit.*

SECOND ATS GIRL. Oh yes, Hilda, I've been thinking.

FIRST ATS GIRL. What about, luv?

SECOND ATS GIRL. You know what I reckon this war's all about?

Long pause.

FIRST ATS GIRL. No.

SECOND ATS GIRL. Just our freedom. To talk to each other.

FIRST ATS GIRL. You want sugar, luv?

DIRECTOR. That was marvellous. Tremendously real. My God, you couldn't do that with actors! All right, Doris. I'm going for a take.

DORIS. Assistant! Get a bit of silence will you?

SON (*moving away from the tea tray*). Sorry Doris . . .

DORIS. Yell 'Quiet' for God's sake.

SON (*moves to the centre of the stage, clears his throat and says very nervously*). Quiet, please!

The noise of the Unit continues.

Can we have a little quiet now, please?

From this moment, the noise intensifies, the CHIPPY *saws at his bit of wood.* SPARKS *sings 'Oh, Salome' and hammers at his 2K. The pontoon game erupts into a loud argument and the two ATS girls start to dance together, humming 'The White Cliffs of Dover'. The light concentrates on the* SON, *fading on the rest of the stage as he becomes more and more panic-stricken.*

SON. We'd appreciate a bit of quiet now, thank you!

Noise.

All quiet now! We're going to try a take.

Noise.

Ladies and gentlemen, will you please give us a little QUIET!

Noise.

QUIET now PLEASE!

There is increased noise. He now sounds hysterical as he yells.

SHUT UP, YOU BASTARDS!

Total silence. Everyone except the SON *quietly leaves the stage, taking with them the paraphernalia of the film unit. The* SON *is left alone. Light change. Upstage a dark girl,* ELIZABETH, *comes in with a chair and sits down to a portable typewriter, puts in paper, lights a cigarette and starts at it. She is dark, beautiful, wearing tight corduroy trousers and a fisherman's sweater.*

SON (*moving towards her*). Is this the writer's department?

The typing continues.

They said I'm not cut out by nature to be an Assistant Director. When I called for 'Quiet' all the electricians went on strike.

The typing continues.

They said with me as an Assistant Director the War'd be over before they finished the movie.

She stops typing, looks up at him and smiles for the first time. Encouraged he goes and looks at what she is typing.

What's the script?

ELIZABETH. It's something Humphrey wants to do. (*She pulls a face.*) There's a character in it called the 'Common Man'. He keeps saying 'Look here, matey, what *is* the World Health Organization?'.
SON. Sounds ghastly.
ELIZABETH (*smiles*). Yes, it is rather.

SON (*sits on the edge of her table*). What on earth do you want to write that for?

ELIZABETH I suppose . . . the school fees.

SON. You studying something?

ELIZABETH (*laughing*). No, you fool. My kids . . . Peter's only got his Captain's pay and . . .

SON. Peter?

ELIZABETH. My husband.

SON (*getting up and moving away from her*). He's abroad?

ELIZABETH. Uxbridge. In Army education.

SON. My father says . . . in time of War you should avoid the temptation to do anything heroic.

ELIZABETH. How odd.

SON. What?

ELIZABETH. What an odd thing for him to say.

SON. You know, after today I think I'll abandon the film business and take up the Law.

Pause. She doesn't react.

My father's a Lawyer.

ELIZABETH. Do you always copy your father?

SON. Good God no!

ELIZABETH. Really? (*She pushes her hair back and looks at him, her long legs stretched out, her hands in her trouser pockets.*) You look the type to agree with Dad.

SON (*looking at her*). There's one thing he says I don't agree with at all.

ELIZABETH. What's that?

> SON *moves to her table. Takes one of her cigarettes, lights it, blows out smoke, doing his best to be elegant and casual.*

SON. He says that sex has been greatly overrated. By the poets . . .

> *Upstage, light fades. Downstage the* FATHER *enters, half-dressed, without his coat, waistcoat or tie. He hooks his braces*

*over his shoulders, shouts, moves round the stage, his hands out
in front of him, groping for the furniture that isn't there.*

FATHER. My tie . . . Oh God in heaven, where's my tie? Will
nobody hand me a waistcoat even? Can't any of you realize the
loneliness of getting dressed?!

The SON *enters with the coat, waistcoat and tie over his arm,
finds the* FATHER'S *wandering hand and puts the tie into it.*

Is that you?

SON. Yes.

FATHER. I suppose you expect me to talk about it.

SON. I know it came as a bit of a shock to you, when Peter
divorced Elizabeth.

FATHER. Must have come as a shock to you too, didn't it? The
fact that she was available for marriage must have rather chilled
your ardour. I mean you're hardly in any state to get married . . .

SON. Do you want to stop us?

FATHER. Are you asking me to? (*Starting to tie his tie without looking.*) How long have you been at the bar, exactly?

SON. Nine months . . .

FATHER. Nine months! I'd been in practise ten years before I felt
the slightest need to marry your mother . . .

SON. Perhaps . . . Needs weren't so urgent then.

FATHER. Got any work have you?

SON. A little work.

FATHER. Unsuccessful defence in a serious case of non renewed
dog licence. That'll hardly keep you in Vim . . .

SON. I don't want to be kept in Vim.

FATHER. But you won't be able to help it – once you're married.
Your no-income will be frittered away on Vim and saucepan
scourers, mansion polish, children's vests and such like
luxuries . . .

SON. I'm quite ready to take on her children.

FATHER. You sound like a railway train. Short stop to take on her

children . . . Waistcoat about anywhere? Yes. In the course of
her life . . . she has acquired children. Mixed blessings I should
imagine, for both of you.

SON. If you're worried about money . . .

FATHER. My dear boy. *I'm* not worried about it. I just think you
haven't bargained for the Vim . . . How long are you going to
deny me my waistcoat?

SON. Here.

> *The* SON *holds out the waistcoat, helps the* FATHER *to struggle
> into it.*

I know you think we're insane . . .

FATHER (*buttoning his waistcoat*). You feel the need to be dis-
suaded.

SON. Of course not. Coat. (*Holding it out.*)

FATHER. I can't help you, you know. (*He struggles into his coat.*)

SON. We don't want help.

FATHER. The children seem lively. As children go. (*Buttoning his
coat.*) Of course it won't be I, who has to keep them in rompers!
I wonder, should I have a drop of Eau-de-Cologne on the handkerchief? I understand your poor girl's coming to tea. We seem
now to be totally surrounded by visitors.

SON. You're not going to be rude to her?

FATHER. Certainly not. Your poor girl and I have got a certain
understanding . . .

SON. For God's sake. Why do you keep calling her my poor
girl?

FATHER. That's really something . . . I'll have to explain to her
after tea.

> *He takes the* SON's *arm. They move off the stage together.*
> ELIZABETH *enters. She waits nervously in the garden area:
> lights a cigarette. The* SON *enters, goes to her quickly, also
> nervous.*

SON. They're just coming . . . (*Pause.*) It's going to be all right.
(*Pause.*) Whatever he says, you won't mind?

ELIZABETH. Will you?

SON. Of course not.

ELIZABETH. *Whatever* he says?

SON. I'm used to it. (*Pause.*) He doesn't mean half of it.

ELIZABETH. I know. But it's difficult. . .

SON. What?

ELIZABETH. Telling which half he means.

The FATHER *enters in his garden hat, his hand on the*
MOTHER's *arm.*

FATHER. Rhododendrons out?

MOTHER. Yes, dear.

FATHER. A fine show of rhododendrons . . . And the little syringa?

MOTHER. Just out.

FATHER. Just out. And smelling sweetly. Azaleas doing well?

MOTHER. You can see they're a little brown, round the edges . . .

FATHER. Azaleas doing moderately well . . . Our visitor here?

MOTHER. Yes, dear. Elizabeth's here.

FATHER. Is that you?

SON. We're both here.

FATHER. Is your visitor enjoying the garden?

ELIZABETH. Very much. Thank you.

FATHER. Good. And is he treating you well?

ELIZABETH. Quite well. Thank you.

FATHER. I've often wondered about my son. Does he treat girls
well . . .?

SON. Why've you wondered that?

FATHER. I once knew a man named Arthur Pennycuick. Like you
in some ways. He didn't treat girls well . . .

MOTHER. Please, dear . . . Arthur Pennycuick's not suitable.

ELIZABETH. Tell us. What did he do to girls?

FATHER. When I was a young man, I was out with this
Pennycuick. And he picked up a girl. In the promenade of the

old Empire Music Hall. And before he went off with her, he took off his cufflinks and gave them to me for safekeeping. In her *presence*! I felt so sick and angry, seeing him take out his old gold cufflinks. I never spoke to him again. Disgusting!

ELIZABETH. You think if you sleep with someone – you should trust them with your cufflinks?

FATHER. At least not take them out – *in front of the girl*! Well, we can see a fine show of rhododendrons.

MOTHER. Yes. And I showed you the polyanthas.

FATHER. A reward at last, for a good deal of tedious potting up.

ELIZABETH (*impatient, as letting out something she's kept bottled up for a long time*). Why do you bother?

FATHER. What?

ELIZABETH. I said why do you bother to do all this gardening? I mean when you can't see it ...

Both the MOTHER *and* SON *try to interrupt her, protectively.*

MOTHER. My dear ...

SON. Elizabeth ...

ELIZABETH. Well he can't see it can he? Why do you all walk about – pretending he's not blind?

The FATHER *shakes off the* MOTHER's *arm and moves, his hand out in front of him, towards* ELIZABETH. *He gets to her: touches her arm, feels down her arm, and puts his in it.*

FATHER. Is that you?

ELIZABETH. Yes ...

FATHER. Would you take me to West Copse? I'd like ... a report on the magnolia. Would you do that? (*Pause.*) Be my eyes.

ELIZABETH looks at him, suspicious, not quite understanding what he's up to. Then she says, almost brutally.

ELIZABETH. Come on then ...

She moves away, with the FATHER *on her arm.*

MOTHER (*looking after* ELIZABETH). She has nice eyes.

SON. Yes.

MOTHER. Not at all the eyes ... of a divorced person.

SON. Does he want to stop us?

MOTHER. Well, it's not easy for him. He's such a household word in Probate, Divorce and Admiralty Division.

SON. Is he going on about that?

MOTHER. No. Not at all.

SON. If he could see her he'd understand why I want to marry her.

MOTHER. Oh, he understands that. (*Smiling.*) I think his main difficulty is understanding why she wants to marry you ...

SON. That's nice of him!

MOTHER (*puts her arm in the* SON's). Would you like to come and help me cut up the oranges? I do hate making marmalade.

SON (*as they move away*). Why not buy it, for God's sake?

MOTHER. He does so enjoy our great annual bout with the marmalade ...

They have now left and the FATHER *and* ELIZABETH *have arrived at a seat in the garden part of the stage.* ELIZABETH *sits the* FATHER *down and sits down beside him.*

FATHER. Come over, did you, in your own small car?
Pause.

ELIZABETH. You've been trying to put him off.

She moves him towards garden seats. Sits down beside him.

FATHER. Not at all.

ELIZABETH. I told him. You'd put him off.

FATHER. He came to me for advice.

ELIZABETH. And I suppose you gave it.

FATHER. I never give advice. It's far too precious. Bit of an asset, don't you find, that private transport?

ELIZABETH. We made up our minds.

FATHER. And your children I believe, are pretty lively. For children ...

ELIZABETH. He gets on marvellously with them . . .

FATHER. And I believe you have your own bits and pieces of furniture. A bedroom suite they tell me. In a fine state of preservation. You're a catch! If you want my honest opinion.

ELIZABETH. Then you ought to be glad for him . . .

FATHER. Him? Look here. Joking apart. You don't want to marry him, do you? I mean he's got no assets . . . of any kind. Not even . . . a kitchen cabinet. And here's another thing about it. (*He takes out a cigar case, removes a cigar.*)

ELIZABETH. What?

FATHER. He won't like it, you know. If you have the flu . . .

ELIZABETH. Really . . .?

FATHER. You see, most people are naturally sympathetic towards illness. They're kind to people with high temperatures. They even cosset them. But not him! He runs a mile. Sneeze once and he'll be off! In the opposite direction!

He puts the unlit cigar in his mouth.

ELIZABETH. I don't get ill all that much . . .

FATHER. But when you do . . . he'll run a mile!

ELIZABETH, I thought it was *me* you might disapprove of . . .

FATHER. Why ever . . .?

ELIZABETH. Think he's marrying someone unsuitable . . .

FATHER. You have particularly nice eyes they tell me.

ELIZABETH. Thanks.

FATHER. And some handsome furniture . . .

ELIZABETH. Not much.

FATHER. And as you told me yourself, your own small runabout.

ELIZABETH. Very bashed.

FATHER. Even so. Not many girls with assets of that description. Couldn't you do better, than someone who bolts if you go two ticks above normal? (*He puts the unlit cigar in his mouth.*)

ELIZABETH. I hadn't thought about it.

FATHER. Oh do think. (*He feels in his pocket, pulls out a box of matches.*) Think carefully! There must be bigger fish than *that* in your own particular sea. (*He strikes a match, holds it some-where in the air.*) You are, I mean, something of a catch.

ELIZABETH *looks at him, smiles, gets up and moves his hand so that the flame lights his cigar.*

You could catch better fish than *that*. I'm prepared to take a bet on it . . . (*He shivers slightly.*) It's getting cold.

ELIZABETH (*gets up, unsmiling*). I'll take you in.

The FATHER *gets up and* ELIZABETH *leads him off the stage. The* SON *enters, wearing a black coat and striped trousers.*

SON (*to the audience*). In that case his advocacy failed. In time he became reconciled to me as a husband for his daughter-in-law.

Pause.

He was right, though. I hadn't bargained for the Vim.

ELIZABETH *enters downstage to the* SON. *She is in a bad mood, stirring something in a pudding bowl.*

ELIZABETH. Made lots of money this week?

SON. Ten guineas. For a divorce.

ELIZABETH. That's marvellous, darling! I had to get them new vests.

SON. What the hell do they do with their vests? In my opinion they eat their vests.

ELIZABETH. And knicker linings. I put them on the account at John Barnes.

SON. The account at John Barnes is assuming the proportions of the National debt.

ELIZABETH. But you ought to be rich.

SON. Ought?

ELIZABETH. I'm up all night. Typing your divorce petitions. They must be paying you – for all those paragraphs of deep humiliation and distress.

SON. You don't get paid for years. In the Law.

ELIZABETH. Can't you ask for it?

SON. Of course I can't.

ELIZABETH. Why not?

SON. You just can't knock on someone's door and say 'What about the ten guineas for the divorce?'

ELIZABETH. I'll go and knock if you like . . .

SON. Anyway, George collects the fees . . .

ELIZABETH. George?

SON. Our clerk. That's his department.

ELIZABETH. He told me his real name's Henry.

SON. My father calls him George.

Light change, upstage a desk. Dim light for the barristers' chambers. GEORGE, *the clerk, dignified, white haired figure with a stiff collar and cuffs comes in, sits down at the desk, opens a drawer, takes out a sandwich and eats.*

ELIZABETH. Whatever for?

SON. Because he once had a clerk called George, who was killed on the Somme . . . So when Henry took over my father went on calling him George.

ELIZABETH. Henry doesn't much like that, if you ask me.

SON. He doesn't mind.

ELIZABETH. You always think no one minds – about your father . .

The SON *moves to her, puts an arm round her shoulder, to cheer her up.*

SON. Let's go to the pub.

ELIZABETH. What on?

SON. The Family Allowance.

ELIZABETH. All right. Shall we play bar billiards?

SON. Like we were doing the night Peter walked in. Remember?

ELIZABETH. And said, 'This is the end of our marriage. I see you've become entirely trivial'.

SON. Do you miss Peter?

ELIZABETH. No. (*Pause, she looks at him.*) Do you?

SON. Of course not.

ELIZABETH. I'm sorry about John Barnes.

SON. That's marriage, isn't it?

ELIZABETH. What's marriage?

SON. An unexpectedly large expenditure on Vim, children's vests and suchlike luxuries . . .

Pause. ELIZABETH *looks at him suspiciously.*

ELIZABETH. Who's that – a quotation from?

Silence. He doesn't answer. They stand for a moment, looking at each other. Upstage, GEORGE *closes the drawer, gets up, takes a hat and umbrella and goes. Downstage* ELIZABETH *and the* SON *go off in different directions; she's still stirring.*

Light change and the SON *re-enters upstage. He looks at the drawers of* GEORGE's *desk. Is tempted. Opens one crack. Peers in. Shuts it when he thinks he hears a noise. Then opens it slowly. Puts in his hand and pulls out a cheque. He looks at the cheque and then whistles with delight. As he is doing so,* GEORGE *re-enters: looks at the* SON *and the open desk drawer and bridles with outrage.*

GEORGE. We have been going, sir, to our personal drawer!

SON. But, George, it's a cheque, for me . . .

GEORGE. We should've given it out to us, sir. In the fullness of time . . .

SON (*kisses the cheque*). Fifteen guineas! Thank God for adultery.

GEORGE. We have never had a gentleman in Chambers that had to grub for money in our personal top drawer . . .

SON. But, George, we're desperately short of Vim.

GEORGE. These things take time, sir.

SON. And what's the point of keeping good money shut up with a box of old pen nibs and a Lyons Individual Fruit Pie. Is it supposed to breed in there or something? (*Pause.*) If you could only get me some more work.

GEORGE. We can't expect much can we? We must wait until a few clients learn to like the cut of our jib.

SON. I've got a talent for divorcing people.

GEORGE. It's not our work. It's our conversation to solicitors that counts. While we're waiting to come on, at London Sessions.

SON. Conversation?

GEORGE. Do we ask them about their tomato plants? Do we remember ourselves to their motor mowers. Do we show a proper concern for their operations and their daughters' figure skating? That's how we rise to heights, in the Law.

SON. My father doesn't do that.

GEORGE. Your father's a case apart.

SON (*rather proud*). My father's obnoxious, to solicitors.

GEORGE (*suddenly shouts*). 'The devil damn thee Black, thou cream faced loon!'

SON (*taken aback*). What?

GEORGE. He said that to Mr Binns, when he'd forgotten to file his affidavit. Your father is something of an exception.

SON. Yes.

GEORGE. I sometimes wonder. Does he realize I'm one of the many Henrys of the world?

SON (*reassuring*). Yes, George. I'm sure he does . . .

Pause. GEORGE *looks at the* SON *more sympathetically.*

GEORGE. Mr Garfield goes down to the Free Legal Centre, Holloway Road. That's where he goes of a Thursday. He picks up the odd guinea or two, on poor persons' cases. And I don't have him in here, sir, ferreting about among my packed meal, sir.

SON. Mr. Garfield lives with his mother – he spends nothing at all on Vim!

GEORGE. He takes the view he might rise to fame from the Free

Legal Centre. He says a murderer might rush in there off the streets any day of the week . . .

Light change. The SON *moves forward and speaks to the audience downstage left. Upstage,* GEORGE *goes. Downstage right, a table and a chair, a portrait of George VI. A* SOCIAL WORKER *with glasses, chain smoking over a pile of files, enters.*

SON. So I went to the Free Legal Centre. To a small room that smelt of old gym shoes and coconut matting where you could hear the distant sounds of billiards and punch ups from the Youth Club and pray that a murderer, still clutching the dripping knife, might burst in from the Holloway Road and beg urgently for Legal Aid.

He turns hopefully to the SOCIAL WORKER.

No murderers in tonight I suppose, Miss Bulstrode?

SOCIAL WORKER. I'm sending you up to my Mr Morrow. I chose you out for him specially.

SON. Why me?

SOCIAL WORKER. He makes Mr Garfield faint.

The SOCIAL WORKER *hands the* SON *a file and goes. The* SON *starts to look at Mr Morrow's file. Change of light upstage and the* FATHER *enters in a black jacket and a light waistcoat, on* GEORGE's *arm.* GEORGE *sits him down at the upstage desk. The* FATHER *lights a cigar and starts to read a page of braille as the* SON *waits for his Free Legal client.*

SON. Back in Chambers my father, smelling of Eau-de-Cologne and occasional cigars, sat among his relics, the blown duck egg on which a client's will had once been written, the caricatures of himself in great cases, the photographs of the signatures in a notorious forgery. He wrote a great textbook on the law of wills . . . becoming expert in the habits of mad old ladies who went fishing for gold under their beds and left all their money to undesirable causes.

FATHER. Let's choose executors and talk of wills.

SON. In the Holloway Road, I waited for more obscure problems.

MR MORROW *comes in downstage to the* SON. *He is an innocent looking, smiling, balding, middle-aged man in a macintosh.*

MR MORROW. Are you the lawyer?

SON. Mr Morrow? Is it matrimonial? (*He opens the file and starts to fill in a form.*)

MR MORROW. Yes, sir. In a sense . . .

SON. You were married on . . .?

MR MORROW. The sixth day of one month. I prefer not to use the heathen notation.

SON. 1940?

MR MORROW. Yes. 1940.

SON. I have to put it down on this form, you see. (*Pause.*) Now – matrimonial offence: I mean, what is the trouble?

MR MORROW. The corpuscles.

SON. There's no place on the Free Legal form for corpuscles.

MR MORROW. Which however, is the trouble . . . That's what I want, sir. The legal position . . . She's on to the red ones, now. I could just about stand it when she only took the white. And my child, sir. My Pamela. I have a very particular respect for that child, who is now losing her hearty appetite.

SON. What's your wife doing exactly?

MR MORROW. She is eating our red corpuscles.

SON. If you're feeling unwell, Mr Morrow. . .

MR MORROW. She drains them from us, by the use of her specs. That is how she drains them out. She focuses her rimless specs upon our bodies, and so our bodies bleed.

SON. Mr Morrow. . .

MR MORROW. I was standing upon the hearth rug, sir, which lies upon my . . . hearth. I looked down between my legs and I saw it there. The scarlet flower. There was the stain of blood on my white fleecy rug sir, red between my legs.

Pause.

SON. Have you spoken to your wife about this at all, Mr Morrow?

MR MORROW. I haven't spoken to her, sir. But she is forgiven. All the same I feel she has let me down. When it was the white she trained her eyes on, sir, it was more or less immaterial. But now she's after my vital strength.

SON. Legally . . .

MR MORROW. A man stands entitled to his own blood, surely. It must be so.

Pause.

SON. I know of no case actually decided, on this particular point.

MR MORROW (*eager*). You're advising me to go to Doncaster, then?

Pause.

SON. You . . . might as well.

MR MORROW. It's your considered and expert opinion, her destructive eye won't be upon me in Doncaster?

SON. Why not try it anyway?

MR MORROW. Very well, sir. I bow to your honest opinion. I shall discontinue all legal proceedings and proceed to Doncaster. Will you require my signature to that effect?

SON. Well, no. I hardly think so.

MR MORROW. That's as well, as it so happens. I never sign, for ethical reasons. (*He moves away.*) It's not the blood I miss, sir. It's the child we have to consider. With all due respect.

He goes. The SON *is left alone. He closes the file and puts it down on the table. Upstage the light increases on the* FATHER *upstage. He repeats loudly.*

FATHER. 'Let's choose executors and talk of wills!'

The SOCIAL WORKER *comes in downstage to the* SON.

SOCIAL WORKER. Mr Morrow looks well contented.

SON. He should. He has absolutely no need of the Law.

The SON *and the* SOCIAL WORKER *go off downstage left.*

FATHER. 'And yet not so . . . For what can we bequeath?
Save our deposed bodies to the ground.
Our land, our lives and all are Bolingbroke's.
And nothing can we call our own but death
And that small model of the barren earth . . .

The SON *enters upstage, hangs up his hat.*

That serves as paste and cover to our bones.'
. . . You're back from lunch.

SON. Yes.

FATHER. You took a long time.

SON. I was talking to a man – he might want to put on my play . . .

FATHER. Possibly you'd work harder if you were a woman barrister.

SON. Possibly . . .

FATHER. I've often said to George, 'Let's have a woman in Chambers'. Women *work* so much harder than men, they can be imposed on so much more easily. Look how seriously girls' schools take lacrosse! They'd treat the law like that. I could get a ridiculous amount of work from a woman pupil.

SON. What does George say?

FATHER (*sad.*) He says there's not the toilet facilities . . . But you know old Carter Davidson once had a woman pupil. He occupied the basement here, rooms easily visible from the garden where the Masters of the Bench stroll, after dinner. Well, they were strolling there, history relates, after a Grand Night with some kind of Royal Personage, King, Queen, Princess . . . something of the kind, and glancing down, what did they see?

SON. Well – what?

FATHER. Carter Davidson and his woman pupil! Naked as puppies, stretched out on the Persian rug. Well, not a word was said, but do you know?

SON. What?

FATHER. Next day Sir Carter Davidson was appointed Chief Justice of the Seaward Isles. They shipped him off, ten thousand miles from the Inns of Court. He couldn't ever understand why. (*Laughs.*) Well, that's one way to get a blooming knighthood . . . Enjoying the Law, are you . . .?

SON. Not all that much.

FATHER. Plays are all very well. Photographs in the paper may be all very fine and large. But you need something real! Hold hard on the law.

SON. Are you sure the Law's real?

FATHER. What on earth do you mean?

SON. No one seems to need it . . . except lawyers . . .

FATHER. The law's not designed for imbeciles, or your friends who combine the art of being called Bill with membership of the female sex. It's not exactly tailor made for the poet Percy Bysshe Shelley . . . No! The whole point of the Law is – it's designed for the ordinary everyday citizen seated aboard the ordinary, everyday Holborn tramcar.

SON. I don't think they have trams in Holborn any more.

FATHER. That's hardly the point.

SON. No trams and no ordinary commonsense citizen sitting on them or anywhere else in the world. They're all busy thinking of the things that really worry them, like the shapes on the ceilings and the stains on the carpet, and they only pretend to be ordinary commonsense citizens when they need lawyers. It's a disguise they put on, like the blue suits and old Boy Scout buttons and the terrible voice they use to take the Bible oath. They're deceiving you, that's what they're doing. They think if they play your game we'll let them off their debts, or order their wives to permit them sexual intercourse, or liberate them from old pointless crimes no one holds against them anyway. All that commonsense legal language we're so proud of – I tell you honestly, it might as well be Chinese . . .

FATHER (*conciliating*). Oh, well now . . . You can get a lot of innocent fun out of the Law. How's your cross?

SON. What?

FATHER. Your cross examination. In Court – have you the makings of a cross examiner?

SON. I don't know.

FATHER. Timing is of great importance. In the art of cross examination.

SON. That's show business.

FATHER. What did you say?

SON. An expression, used by actors.

FATHER (*without interest*). Really? How interesting. Now I always count, in silence of course, up to forty-three before starting a cross examination.

SON. Whatever for?

FATHER. The witness imagines you're thinking up some utterly devastating question.

SON. And are you?

FATHER. Of course not. I'm just counting. Up to forty-three. However, it unnerves the gentleman in the box. Then, start off with the knock out! Don't leave it till the end; go in with your guns blazing! Ask him . . .

SON. What?

FATHER. Is there anything in your conduct, Mr Nokes, of which, looking back on it, you now feel heartily *ashamed*?

SON. Is that a good question?

FATHER. It's an excellent question!

SON. Why exactly?

FATHER. Because if he says 'yes' he's made an admission, and if he says 'no' he's a self-satisfied idiot and he's lost the sympathy of the Court.

SON. Anything else?

FATHER. Say you've got a letter in which he admits something discreditable . . . like, well having apologised to his wife for instance . . . Now then, how're you going to put that to him?

SON. Did you, or did you not . . .

FATHER. Not bad.

SON. Write a letter apologising to your wife?

FATHER. Well, I suppose you're young.

SON. Isn't that right?

FATHER. Not what I should call the *art* of cross examination.

SON. So how . . .?

FATHER. You be Nokes.

SON. All right.

FATHER. You behaved disgracefully to your wife, did you not?

SON. No.

FATHER. In fact, so disgracefully that you had to apologise to her.

SON. I don't remember.

FATHER. Will you swear you did not?

SON. What?

FATHER. Will you swear you didn't apologise to her?

SON. All right.

FATHER. Now please turn to the letter on page 23. Just read it out to us will you?

SON. I see. (*Pause*). What's the point of all this actually?

FATHER (*standing up, very positive*). The point. My dear boy, the point is to do down your opponent. To obliterate whoever's agin you. That's what the point of it is . . . And of course, to have a bit of fun, while you're about it.

Tapping with his stick, the FATHER, *feels his way off. The* SON *moves down stage and speaks to the audience.*

SON. My father got too old for the train journey to London . . .
A ROBING ROOM MAN *comes in with a wig and gown, stand up collar and bands, and stands by the* SON. *As he speaks the* SON *unfixes his own collar, hands it to the man, takes the collar which is handed to him, puts it on, ties the bands and is robed in the wig and gown. Upstage Courtroom arches are projected, a* JUDGE *is sitting in wig and gown. A* LADY WITNESS, *in a flowered hat and gloves is waiting to be questioned.*

My father retired on a pension of nothing but credit, optimism and determination not to think of anything unpleasant. His money had gone on cigars and barrels of oysters and Eau-de Cologne for his handkerchief and always first class on the railway and great rare Japanese cherry trees that rustled in the wind and flowered for two weeks a year in a green-white shower he never saw. He left to me all the subtle pleasures of the law . . .

JUDGE (*loudly to the* SON). Do you want to cross examine this witness?

SON (*turns round as if woken from a reverie and enters the Court-room scene*). Certainly, my Lord.

JUDGE. Very well, get on with it.

SON (*turns to the witness*). Now madam . . .

WITNESS. Yes.

SON (*starting on a menacing pause, he begins to count under his breath*). One . . . two . . . three . . . four . . . five . . . six . . . seven . . . eight . . . nine . . .

JUDGE. Are you intending to *ask* any questions?

SON. Twelve . . . thirteen . . . I'm sorry, my Lord . . .?

JUDGE. If you've got a question to ask, ask it. We can't all wait while you stand in silent prayer you know.

Offstage, sound of laughter.

SON. I'm sorry my Lord . . . Now, madam. Is there anything you've ever done you're ashamed of?

WITNESS. Yes.

SON. Ah. And what're you ashamed of?

WITNESS. I once wrote up for an autograph . . . with picture. You know the type of thing. At my age! Well I began off 'Am heartily ashamed to write up but –'

JUDGE. Have you any *relevant* questions?

SON. Will you please read this letter? The one I am about to hand you . . .

WITNESS. Oh, yes.

SON. Read it out to us, please.

WITNESS. I can't . . .

SON. Madam. The Court is waiting . . .

WITNESS. I really can't.

SON. Is there something there you'd rather not remember?

WITNESS. Not exactly . . .

SON (*very severe*). Then read it, madam!

WITNESS. Could I borrow your glasses?

Laughter.

The laughter fades. Light change as the SON *goes. The* MOTHER *is laying the dinner table. The* FATHER's *in his arm chair, his eyes closed, apparently asleep. A small table with a portable radio on it.* ELIZABETH *enters, exhausted from putting the children to bed. She and the* MOTHER *talk quietly, not to wake up the* FATHER.

MOTHER. Are the children settled?

ELIZABETH (*lighting a cigarette*). Yes. They're all settled.

MOTHER. How's our little Jennifer?

ELIZABETH. Your little Jennifer's fine. (*She starts to help her lay.*) And so are our Daniel and Jonathon.

MOTHER. Jenny's so pretty. I'd like to have done a drawing of her. Perhaps a crayon . . .

ELIZABETH. Why don't you?

MOTHER (*laughs at the ridiculousness of the idea*). Oh, I gave up drawing when I got married. You have to don't you – give up things when you get married . . .

ELIZABETH. Do you?

MOTHER. And of course there's no time now . . .

ELIZABETH (*looks at the* FATHER *and whispers*). Doesn't he leave you half an hour to yourself?

MOTHER (*whispers*). He doesn't like to be left. I suppose . . . I often think. (*She pauses with a handful of cutlery.*) Someday I'll be alone shan't I. You can't help thinking.

Pause. ELIZABETH *looks at her.*

ELIZABETH. (*whispers*). What'll you do? Travel. Go to France.

MOTHER. Oh no. I shall stay here of course. Somebody has to see to the marmalade.

> *She puts down the handful of cutlery and determinedly goes on laying. Sound of a car stopping.* ELIZABETH *looks out, as if from a window.*

ELIZABETH. There he is – come to join the family for the week-end.

MOTHER. It seems they're giving him a lot of briefs now.

ELIZABETH. Yes.

MOTHER. It's hard to believe. (*Pause.*) It must be keeping you very busy.

ELIZABETH. Me? Why me?

MOTHER. Don't you help him – with his cases?

ELIZABETH. He's got a secretary now. He hardly ever discusses his work: he thinks I take it too seriously.

MOTHER. Of course his father misses going to London – He used to get such a lot of fun, out of the divorces . . .

FATHER (*opening his eyes*). What's that?

MOTHER. I said you missed going to London, dear.

FATHER. It's my son, you know. He's pinched all my work.

> *The* SON *enters carrying a bottle of champagne.*

SON. Victory!

ELIZABETH. What's happened, darling?

SON. I won . . . Timson *v* Timson. After five days.

FATHER (*smacking his lips*). Five refreshers!

SON. They insisted on fighting every inch of the way. Terribly litigious . . .

FATHER. The sort to breed from – those Timsons!

SON. I brought champagne. For a small celebration.

> *He starts to open the champagne.*

ELIZABETH (*mutters*). Just like a wedding.

SON. What did you say?

ELIZABETH. Oh nothing.

SON (*pours a glass of champagne. Gives it to the* MOTHER).
Champagne . . .

MOTHER. How festive. Isn't it festive, dear?

The SON *is handing a glass to the* FATHER.

FATHER. What is?

MOTHER. He's handing you a glass of champagne.

FATHER. I'm glad you can afford such things, old boy. Now that
you've pinched all my practice. (*He drinks.*) I suppose you're
polite to solicitors?

SON. Occasionally.

FATHER. I could never bring myself . . . Pity. If I'd gone to dinner
with solicitors I might've had something to leave you – over and
above my overdraft. I remember after one case, on The Temple
Station, my solicitor said, 'Are you going West, dear boy, we
might have dinner together'. 'No' I lied to him, I was so
anxious to get away. 'I'm going East.' I ended up with a sandwich in Bethnal Green. It's been my fault . . . The determination
– to be alone. (*He drinks.*) You know what'd go very nicely with
this champagne?

MOTHER. What, dear – a biscuit?

FATHER. No. The crossword.

The MOTHER *sits beside the* FATHER *and opens* The Times. *The*
SON *pours champagne for* ELIZABETH. *She turns on the radio,*
they drink. The radio starts to play an early Elvis Presley. The
SON *and* ELIZABETH *start to dance together: a slow jive.*

MOTHER. The N.C.O. sounds agony.

FATHER. How many words?

MOTHER. Two. Eight and ten.

FATHER. Corporal Punishment.

MOTHER. How clever!

FATHER. Oh, I've got this crossword fellow at my mercy.

ELIZABETH. You're very clever, darling.

SON. Yes.

Pause.

ELIZABETH. The only thing is . . .

SON. What?

ELIZABETH. I thought . . . I mean in that Timson *v* Timson. Weren't you for the husband?

SON. Of course I was for the husband.

ELIZABETH. Wasn't he the man who insisted on his wife tickling the soles of his feet. Four hours at a stretch . . .

SON. It was only while they watched television.

ELIZABETH. With a contraption! A foot tickler . . .?

SON. Something he improvised. With a system of weights and pulleys. It was ingenious actually. The work was done with an old pipe cleaner.

Pause.

ELIZABETH *(Puzzled)*. *Ought* he to have won?

SON *(correcting her)*. *I* won.

ELIZABETH. But *ought* you . . .?

SON. The Judge said it was part of the wear and tear of married life.

ELIZABETH. Yes, but how did *they* feel about it. I mean, I suppose they're still married, aren't they?

SON. They looked a little confused.

ELIZABETH. Perhaps they didn't appreciate the rules of the game.

SON. I enjoyed it . . .

The music stops. They stand facing each other.

ELIZABETH. You enjoy playing games?

SON. I . . . I suppose so.

ELIZABETH. You know what?

SON. What?

ELIZABETH *(quite loudly)*. You get more like him. Every day.

The FATHER *looks up.*

FATHER. Isn't it time we had dinner?
MOTHER. It's all ready.

She moves with the FATHER *to the table. From the other side of the stage the* SON *and* ELIZABETH *move towards the table.*

ELIZABETH. Will he try and start arguments at dinner?

The FATHER *and* MOTHER *sit down at the dining table.*

SON. Of course.
ELIZABETH. Why?
SON. Because that's what he enjoys.

They sit down at the table too. An awkward silence, which the FATHER *breaks.*

FATHER. Music! I can't imagine anyone actually *liking* music.

Pause.

The immortality of the soul! What a boring conception! Can't think of anything worse than living for infinity in a great transcendental hotel, with nothing to do in the evenings . . .

Pause.

What's the time?
MOTHER. Half past eight.
FATHER. Ah! The time's nipping along nicely. (*Pause.*) Nothing narrows the mind so much as foreign travel. Stay at home. That's the way to see the world.
ELIZABETH. I don't know that's true.
FATHER. Of course it's true! And I'll tell you something else, Elizabeth. Just between the two of us. There's a lot of sorry stuff in D. H. Lawrence.
ELIZABETH. I don't know about that either.
FATHER. Oh yes there is. And a lot of damned dull stuff in old Proust. (*Pause.*) Did you hear that, Elizabeth? Lot of damned dull stuff in old Proust.

ELIZABETH. Yes. I heard.

FATHER. I'll say one thing for you . . . At least you're an improvement on the ones he used to bring home. Girls that would closet themselves in the bathroom for hours on end. And nothing to show for it . . . None of them lasted long.

ELIZABETH. I wonder why?

FATHER. Yes. I wonder. At least my son's someone to talk to. Most people get damned dull children.

The SON *fills his glass. The* FATHER *puts his hand out, feels the* SON's *hand.*

Is that you?

SON. Yes.

FATHER. Your play came across quite well they told me.

SON. Yes.

Pause.

MOTHER. Won't you have one of my little tarts?

Pause.

FATHER. I see that other fellow's play got very good notices. You want to watch out he doesn't put your nose out of joint.

Pause.

I haven't been sleeping lately.

Pause.

And sometimes when I can't sleep, you know, I like to make a list of all the things I really hate.

MOTHER. Do have one of my little tarts, Elizabeth.

ELIZABETH. Is it a long list?

FATHER. Not very. Soft eggs. Cold plates. Waiting for things. Parsons.

SON. Parsons?

FATHER. Yes. Parsons. On the wireless. If those fellows bore God as much as they bore me, I'm sorry for Him . . .

ELIZABETH. My father's a parson.
FATHER. I know. (*Pause.*) 'Nymph, in thy orisons be all my sins
remembered.'

Pause. He smacks at the air with his hand.

Is that a wasp?
MOTHER. Yes, dear.
FATHER. What's it doing?
MOTHER. It's going away.
FATHER. After you've been troubled by a wasp, don't you love a
fly?

Pause.

Don't the evenings seem terribly long now you're married?
Aren't you finding it tremendously tedious? What do you do
– have wireless?
ELIZABETH. We don't get bored, exactly.
SON. We can always quarrel.
FATHER. I was surprised to hear about that play of yours.
SON. Were you?
FATHER. When you told us the story of that play, I said 'Ha. Ha.
This is a bit thin. This is rather poor fooling'. Didn't I say that?
MOTHER. Yes, dear.
FATHER. 'This is likely to come very tardy off.' But now it appears
to have come across quite well. Didn't that surprise you,
Elizabeth?
ELIZABETH. Well . . .
SON. She doesn't like it.
FATHER. What?
SON. Elizabeth doesn't like it very much.
FATHER (*interested*). Really? That's interesting. Now tell me
why . . .

Pause.

ELIZABETH. Not serious.

FATHER. You don't think so? You think he's not serious.

ELIZABETH. He plays games. He makes jokes. When the time comes to say anything serious it's as if . . .

SON. Oh for heaven's sake!

FATHER. Go on.

ELIZABETH. There was something stopping him. All the time . . .

FATHER. Is that true? I wonder why that is . . .

ELIZABETH. I should think you'd know.

FATHER. Why?

ELIZABETH. Because you've never really said anything serious to him, have you? No one here ever says anything . . . They make jokes . . . and tell stories . . . and . . . something's *happening*!

SON. Elizabeth. It doesn't always have to be said.

ELIZABETH. Sometimes. Sometimes it has to.

FATHER. All right. What would you like to hear me say? What words . . .of wisdom?

Silence. They look at him. No one says anything. Very softly he starts to sing.

FATHER (*sings*). 'She was as beeootiful
                 As a butterfly
                 And proud as a queen
                 Was pretty little Polly Perkins
                 Of Paddington Green . . .'

The SON *gets up from the table and moves forward towards the audience. Light fades on the upstage area, where the* FATHER, MOTHER *and* ELIZABETH *go.*

SON (*to the audience*). He had no message. I think he had no belief. He was the advocate who can take the side that comes to him first and always discover words to anger his opponent. He was the challenger who flung his glove down in the darkness and waited for an argument. And when the children came to see him he told them no more, and no less, than he'd told to me . . .

THREE CHILDREN *run in. Two boys and a girl, dressed in jeans and sweaters. They take packets of mints out of the* FATHER's *waistcoat pocket, pull out his gold watch, blow on it and he makes it open miraculously for them.*

FATHER. Who's this?

GIRL. Daniel . . .

FATHER. Oh really. And you're . . .

FIRST BOY. I'm Jennifer . . .

GIRL. I'm Daniel. Honestly.

SECOND BOY. She's a liar.

FATHER. Oh come now. If she says she's Daniel – shouldn't we take her word for it?

FIRST BOY. Tell us some more . . .

FATHER. What about?

SECOND BOY. The Macbeths . . .

GIRL (*with relish*). The Macbeths!

> *They sit down, look up at him. The* FATHER *starts to tell the story. The* SON, *downstage, looks on.*

FATHER. Dunsinane! What a dreadful place to stay . . . for the weekend. Draughts. No hot water. No wireless! The alarm bell going off in the night just when you least expected it. And finally . . . The dinner party!

CHILDREN. Go on! Tell us! Tell us about the dinner party! (*etc.*)

FATHER. A most embarrassing affair. Dinner with the Macbeths. And everyone's sitting down . . . quite comfortable. And his wife says 'Come and sit down, dear. The soup's getting cold . . .' And he turns to his chair and sees . . . (*He points with a trembling, terrible finger.*) Someone . . . Something, horrible! Banquo . . . (*His voice sinks to a terrifying whisper.*)

'The time has been
That, when the brains were out the man would die,
And there an end; but now they rise again
With twenty mortal murders on their crowns,

And push us from our stools . . .'
He grabs the GIRL *by the arm. The* CHILDREN *are roaring with laughter.*

SON. I used to scream when he did that to me.
The CHILDREN *become quiet again. The* FATHER *is talking to them, telling them stories. They are listening.*

(*To the audience.*) His mind was full of the books he read as a boy, lying in the hot fields in his prickly Norfolk Jacket. He told them about foggy afternoons in Baker Street and sabres at dawn at Spardau Castle, and Umslopagas and Alan Quartermaine and She Who Must Be Obeyed. He spoke to them of the absurdities of his life . . .

FATHER. My old father was a great one for doing unwelcome acts of kindness! Recall his rash conduct in the affair of my Uncle George's dog . . .

During this story which the CHILDREN *know by heart, they prompt him.*

FIRST BOY. It's the dog . . .!
SECOND BOY. Go on about the dog.
GIRL. Uncle George's Dog . . .
FATHER. My poor Uncle George fell on evil days . . . and had to sell his faithful pointer. And my father, thinking he was heartbroken, went furtively about . . . to buy the animal back. It was a most . . .
GIRL. Lugubrious hound?
FATHER. With a long powerful rudder! It seldom or never smiled. It was not so much dangerous as . . .
FIRST BOY. Depressing?
FATHER. Depressing indeed! And as soon as he saw it, my Uncle George went off to Uxbridge where he had taken a post with good prospects and diggings at which animals were unfortunately not permitted . . . He shed no tears, to my old father's

surprise, at parting from his dumb friend who then took up residence with us. (*He starts to laugh.*) A most . . .

GIRL. Unwelcome guest . . .'

FATHER. Now at that time my brother conducted evening classes. In Pitman's shorthand! And the dog used to crouch at the corner of the house by night and when my brother's pupils arrived he foolishly mistook them for burglars and sprang out at them! Our house happened to be built on a sort of low cliff, and more than one of the students dropped off the edge of the cliff and was (*Laughing loudly.*) badly hurt!

> *Upstage* ELIZABETH *enters, stands looking at the* FATHER *and the* CHILDREN.

ELIZABETH. We must get back. We must really.

CHILDREN. No, Mummy. It's the one about the dog . . . Let's finish the dog. (*etc.*)

FATHER (*laughing, the* CHILDREN *begin to laugh with him*). My brother's shorthand lessons became unpopular. (*Laughs.*) We offered the dog to anyone who'd provide a good home for it. Then we said we'd be content with a thoroughly bad home for the dog. (*Laughs.*) We offered the dog to anyone who'd provide a good home for it. Then we said we'd be content with a thoroughly bad home for the dog. (*Laughs.*) Finally we had to pay the owner a large sum of money to take the animal back. (*Laughs.*) But my mother and I used to remember terrible stories – about faithful hounds who were able to find their way home . . . (*He laughs uncontrollably as the* CHILDREN *pull him to his feet and join him in shouting the last line of the story.*)

FATHER AND CHILDREN. *Over immense distances!*

ELIZABETH. Come on now. We must go, really.

> *The* MOTHER *comes in, takes the* FATHER's *arm. They stand waving as* ELIZABETH *and the* CHILDREN *go off, shouting 'Goodbye', 'Goodbye'. Then when* ELIZABETH *and the* CHILDREN *have gone, the* FATHER *and* MOTHER *turn and go on the other side of the stage.*

Light change. Projection of the garden. Weedy and overgrown. Sound of wind.

SON. The enormous garden became dark and overgrown in spreading patches. He continued, every day, to chronicle its progress in the diary he dictated.

Offstage voice, amplified, the FATHER *speaks.*

FATHER. Put sodium chlorate on the front path. We had raspberry pie from our own raspberries. The dahlias are coming into flower. The jays are eating all the peas . . .

SON. Willow herb and thistles and bright poppies grew up. The fruit cage collapsed like a shaken temple and woods supported the tumbled netting. The rhododendrons and yew hedges grew high as a jungle, tall and dark and uncontrolled, lit with unexpected flowers . . .

FATHER (*O.S.*). Thomas came and we saw him standing still among the camellias . . .

SON. A boy was hired to engage the garden in single combat. His name was not Thomas.

FATHER (*O.S.*). Planted a hundred white crocus and staked up the Malva Alcoa. A dragon fly came into the sitting room. Thomas was paid. Am laid up. The pest officer arrived to eliminate the wasp nests. Unhappily I couldn't watch the destruction . . .

SON. In the summer, with the garden at its most turbulent, he became suddenly very old and ill . . .

ELIZABETH (*O.S.*). 'What are you going to take for breakfast, Mr Phelps?' said Holmes, 'Curried fowl, eggs or will you help yourself?'

Change of light upstage. The FATHER *is in bed.* ELIZABETH *is sitting at his bedside, reading to him. On the other side of the bed, there is an oxygen cylinder and a mask.*

ELIZABETH. 'Thank you, I can eat nothing,' said Phelps. 'Oh come. Try the dish before you.' 'Thank you, I would really

rather not.' 'Well then' said Holmes, with a mischievous twinkle
'I suppose you have no objections to helping me?'

The FATHER *is gasping, breathing with great difficulty.*
ELIZABETH *goes on reading.*

'Phelps raised the cover, and as he did so, uttered a scream, and
sat there staring with his face as white as the plate upon which
he looked. Across the centre of it was lying a little cylinder of
blue-grey paper . . .'

FATHER (*gasps*). The Naval Treaty!

ELIZABETH. Yes.

FATHER. I'm afraid . . . you find that story a great bore.

ELIZABETH. Of course not. It was very exciting.

FATHER. Dear . . . Elizabeth. I'm so glad to discover . . . you can
lie as mercifully as anyone . . .

The SON *moves upstage to the bed.* ELIZABETH *gets up and
goes. The* SON *sits down beside the bed. Pause. The* FATHER's
*breathing is irregular. Then, with a sudden effort, he tries to get
out of bed.*

I want a bath! Get them to take me to the bathroom. Cretins!

The SON *holds him. Pushes him gently back into bed.*

SON. Lie still. Don't be angry.

FATHER (*back in bed, gasping*). I'm always angry – when I'm
dying.

*His breathing becomes more irregular. Stops altogether for a
moment when the* SON *grabs the oxygen mask and puts it on his
face. There's a sound of loud, rasping, regular, oxygen-assisted
breath. The light and projections change to night.*

SON. It was a hot endless night, in a small house surrounded by a
great garden in which all the plants were on the point of mutiny.

Long pause. The breathing continues. The SON *gets up, stands, looks down at his* FATHER *who is now sleeping. The* DOCTOR *comes in. He is in a dinner jacket. He nods to the* SON *and leans over the* FATHER.

SON. Dr Ellis . . .

DOCTOR. We've got a territorial dinner. In High Wycombe . . .

SON. How is he?

DOCTOR. Wake up! Wake up! (*To* SON.) Don't let him sleep. That's the great thing. Wakey wakey! That's better . . .

SON. But do you think . . .?

DOCTOR. The only thing to do is to keep his eyes open. There's really nothing else. I've spoken to your mother. (*Pause.*) I'll come back in the morning.

The DOCTOR *goes. The* SON *turns back to the bed. Looks at the* FATHER. *Sits on the bed and speaks urgently.*

SON. Wake up! Please! Please! Wake up!

The oxygen breathing mounts to a climax and stops. Silence. The SON *gets up slowly. Slowly the light fades upstage and, as it is in darkness, the* SON *moves downstage and speaks to the audience.*

SON. I'd been told of all the things you're meant to feel. Sudden freedom, growing up, the end of dependence, the step into the sunlight when no one is taller than you and you're in no one else's shadow.

Pause.

I know what I felt. Lonely.

He turns and slowly walks away. The stage is empty. And then becomes brilliantly lit, the back wall covered with projections of the garden in full flower.

THE END

The Dock Brief

First produced by the BBC Third Programme on May 12, 1957. The cast was as follows:

MORGENHALL   *Michael Hordern*
FOWLE   *David Kosoff*

Produced by Nesta Pain

On September 16, 1957 the play was produced on BBC television with the same cast and producer.

Michael Codron with David Hall (for Talbot Productions Ltd.) presented the play in a double bill (with *What Shall We Tell Caroline?*) at the Lyric Opera House, Hammersmith, on April 9, 1958, and on May 20, 1958 at the Garrick Theatre. The cast was as follows:

MORGENHALL   *Michael Hordern*
FOWLE   *Maurice Denham*

Directed by Stuart Burge
Designed by Disley Jones

Scene One

*A cell. The walls are grey and fade upwards into the shadows, so
that the ceiling is not seen, and it might even be possible to escape
upwards. The door is right. Back stage is a high, barred window
through which the sky looks very blue. Under the window is a stool.
Against the left wall is a bench with a wooden cupboard next to it.
On the cupboard a wash basin, a towel and a Bible.*

*A small fat prisoner is standing on the stool on tip toes, his hands
in his pockets. His eyes are on the sky.*

Bolts shoot back. The door opens. MORGENHALL *strides in.
He is dressed in a black gown and bands, an aged barrister with
the appearance of a dusty vulture. He speaks off stage, to the
warder.*

MORGENHALL (*to an unseen warder*). Is this where . . . you
keep Mr Fowle? Good, excellent. Then leave us alone like a
kind fellow. Would you mind closing the door? These old
places are so draughty.

> *The door closes. The bolts shoot back.*

Mr Fowle . . . Where are you, Mr Fowle? Not escaped, I
pray. Good Heavens man, come down. Come down, Mr
Fowle.

> *He darts at him and there is a struggle as he pulls down the
> bewildered* FOWLE.

I haven't hurt you?
FOWLE: *negative sounding noise.*

I was suddenly anxious. A man in your unfortunate position.
Desperate measures. And I couldn't bear to lose you . . . No,
don't stand up. It's difficult for you without braces, or a belt,

I can see. And no tie, no shoe-laces. I'm so glad they're looking after you. You must forgive me if I frightened you just a little, Mr Fowle. It was when I saw you up by that window. . . .

FOWLE (*a hoarse and sad voice*). Epping Forest.

MORGENHALL. What did your say?

FOWLE. I think you can see Epping Forest.

MORGENHALL. No doubt you can. But why, my dear chap, why should you want to?

FOWLE. It's the home stretch.

MORGENHALL. Very well.

FOWLE. I thought I could get a glimpse of the green. Between the chimneys and that shed. . . .

FOWLE *starts to climb up again. A brief renewed struggle.*

MORGENHALL. No, get down. It's not wise to be up there, forever trying to look out. There's a draughty, sneeping wind. Treacherous.

FOWLE. Treacherous?

MORGENHALL. I'm afraid so. You never know what a mean, sneeping wind can do. Catch you by the throat, start a sneeze, then a dry tickle on the chest. I don't want anything to catch you like that before . . .

FOWLE. Before what?

MORGENHALL. You're much better sitting quietly down there in the warm. Just sit quietly and I'll introduce myself.

FOWLE. I am tired.

MORGENHALL. I'm Wilfred Morgenhall.

FOWLE. Wilfred?

MORGENHALL. Morgenhall. The barrister.

FOWLE. The barrister?

MORGENHALL. Perfectly so. . . .

FOWLE. I'm sorry.

MORGENHALL. Why?

FOWLE. A barrister. That's very bad.

MORGENHALL. I don't know. Why's it so bad?

FOWLE. When a gentleman of your stamp goes wrong. A long fall.

MORGENHALL. What can you mean?

FOWLE. Different for an individual like me. I only kept a small seed shop.

MORGENHALL. Seed shop? My poor fellow. We mustn't let this unfortunate little case confuse us. We're going to remain very calm, very lucid. We're going to come to important decisions. Now, do me a favour, Mr Fowle, no more seed shops.

FOWLE. Birdseed, of course. Individuals down our way kept birds mostly. Canaries and budgies. The budgies talked. Lot of lonely people down our way. They kept them for the talk.

MORGENHALL. Mr Fowle. I'm a barrister.

FOWLE. Tragic.

MORGENHALL. I know the law.

FOWLE. It's trapped you.

MORGENHALL. I'm here to help you.

FOWLE. We'll help each other.

Pause.

MORGENHALL (*laughs uncontrollably*). I see. Mr Fowle. I see where you've been bewildered. You think I'm in trouble as well. Then I've got good news for you at last. I'm free. Oh yes. I can leave here when I like.

FOWLE. You can?

MORGENHALL. The police are my friends.

FOWLE. They are?

MORGENHALL. And I've never felt better in my life. There now. That's relieved you, hasn't it? I'm not in any trouble.

FOWLE. Family all well?

MORGENHALL. I never married.

FOWLE. Rent paid up?

MORGENHALL. A week or two owing perhaps. Temporary lull in business. This case will end all that.

FOWLE. Which case?

MORGENHALL. Your case.

FOWLE. My . . . ?

MORGENHALL. Case.

FOWLE. Oh that – it's not important.

MORGENHALL. Not?

FOWLE. I don't care about it to any large extent. Not as at present advised.

MORGENHALL. Mr Fowle. How could you say that?

FOWLE. The flavour's gone out of it.

MORGENHALL. But we're only at the beginning.

FOWLE. I can't believe it's me concerned. . . .

MORGENHALL. But it is you, Mr Fowle. You mustn't let yourself forget that. You see, that's why you're here. . . .

FOWLE. I can't seem to bother with it.

MORGENHALL. Can you be so busy?

FOWLE. Slopping in, slopping out. Peering at the old forest. It fills in the day.

MORGENHALL. You seem, if I may say so, to have adopted an unpleasantly selfish attitude.

FOWLE. Selfish?

MORGENHALL. Dog in the manger.

FOWLE. In the?

MORGENHALL. Unenthusiastic.

FOWLE. You're speaking quite frankly, I well appreciate. . . .

MORGENHALL. I'm sorry, Fowle. You made me say it. There's so much of this about nowadays. There's so much ready made entertainment. Free billiards, National Health. Television. There's not the spirit abroad there used to be.

FOWLE. You feel that?

MORGENHALL. Whatever I've done I've always been mustard keen on my work. I've never lost the vision, Fowle. In all my disappointments I've never lost the love of the job.

FOWLE. The position in life you've obtained to.

MORGENHALL. Years of study I had to put in. It didn't just drop in my lap.

FOWLE. I've never studied. . . .

MORGENHALL. Year after year, Fowle, my window at college was alight until two a.m. There I sat among my books. I fed mainly on herrings. . . .

FOWLE. Lean years?

MORGENHALL. And black tea. No subsidized biscuits then, Fowle, no County Council tobacco, just work. . . .

FOWLE. Book work, almost entirely? I'm only assuming that, of course.

MORGENHALL. Want to hear some Latin?

FOWLE. Only if you have time.

MORGENHALL. Actus non sit reus nisi mens sit rea. Filius nullius. In flagrante delicto. Understand it?

FOWLE. I'm no scholar.

MORGENHALL. You most certainly are not. But I had to be, we all had to be in my day. Then we'd sit for the examinations, Mods, Smalls, Greats, Tripos, Little Goes, week after week, rowing men fainting, Indian students vomiting with fear, and no creeping out for a peep at the book under the pretext of a pump ship or getting a glance at the other fellow's celluloid cuff. . . .

FOWLE. That would be unheard of?

MORGENHALL. Then weeks, months of waiting. Nerve racking. Go up to the Lake District. Pace the mountains, play draughts, forget to huff. Then comes the fatal post-card.

FOWLE. What's it say?

MORGENHALL. Satisfied the examiners.

FOWLE. At last!

MORGENHALL. Don't rejoice so soon. True enough I felt I'd turned a corner, got a fur hood, bumped on the head with a

Bible. Bachelor of Law sounded sweet in my ears. I thought of celebrating, a few kindred spirits round for a light ale. Told the only lady in my life that in five years' time perhaps . . .

FOWLE. You'd arrived!

MORGENHALL. That's what I thought when they painted my name up on my London chambers. I sat down to fill in the time until they sent my first brief in a real case. I sat down to do the crossword puzzle while I waited. Five years later, Fowle, what was I doing . . . ?

FOWLE. A little charge of High Treason?

MORGENHALL. I was still doing the crossword puzzle.

FOWLE. But better at it?

MORGENHALL. Not much. Not very much. As the years pass there come to be clues you no longer understand.

FOWLE. So all that training?

MORGENHALL. Wasted. The talents rust.

FOWLE. And the lady?

MORGENHALL. Drove an ambulance in the 1914. A stray piece of shrapnel took her. I don't care to talk of it.

FOWLE. Tragic

MORGENHALL. What was?

FOWLE. Tragic my wife was never called up.

MORGENHALL. You mustn't talk like that, Fowle, your poor wife.

FOWLE. Don't let's carry on about me.

MORGENHALL. But we must carry on about you. That's what I'm here for.

FOWLE. You're here to?

MORGENHALL. Defend you.

FOWLE. Can't be done.

MORGENHALL. Why ever not?

FOWLE. I know who killed her.

MORGENHALL. Who?

FOWLE. Me.

Pause

MORGENHALL (*considerable thought before he says*). Mr Fowle,
I have all the respect in the world for your opinions, but we
must face this. You're a man of very little education. . . .

FOWLE. That's true.

MORGENHALL. One has only to glance at you. At those
curious lobes to your ears. At the line of your hair. At the
strange way your eyebrows connect in the middle, to see that
you're a person of very limited intelligence.

FOWLE. Agreed, quite frankly.

MORGENHALL. You think you killed your wife.

FOWLE. Seems to me.

MORGENHALL. Mr Fowle. Look at yourself objectively. On
questions of birdseed I have no doubt you may be infallible –
but on a vital point like this might you not be mistaken. . . .
Don't answer . . .

FOWLE. Why not, sir?

MORGENHALL. Before you drop the bomb of a reply, consider
who will be wounded. Are the innocent to suffer?

FOWLE. I only want to be honest.

MORGENHALL. But you're a criminal, Mr Fowle. You've
broken through the narrow fabric of honesty. You are free
to be kind, human, to do good.

FOWLE. But what I did to her . . .

MORGENHALL. She's passed, you know, out of your life.
You've set up new relationships. You've picked out me.

FOWLE. Picked out?

MORGENHALL. Selected.

FOWLE. But I didn't know. . . .

MORGENHALL. No, Mr Fowle. That's the whole beauty of it.
You didn't know me. You came to me under a system of
chance invented, like the football pools, to even out the
harsh inequality of a world where you have to deserve
success. You, Mr Fowle, are my first Dock Brief.

FOWLE. Your Dock?

MORGENHALL. Brief.

FOWLE. You couldn't explain?

MORGENHALL. Of course. Prisoners with no money and no friends exist. Luckily, you're one of them. They're entitled to choose any barrister sitting in Court to defend them. The barrister, however old, gets a brief, and is remunerated on a modest scale. Busy lawyers, wealthy lawyers, men with other interests, creep out of Court bent double when the Dock Brief is chosen. We regulars who are not busy sit on. I've been a regular for years. It's not etiquette, you see, even if you want the work, to wave at the prisoner, or whistle, or try to catch his eye by hoisting any sort of little flag.

FOWLE. Didn't know.

MORGENHALL. But you *can* choose the most advantageous seat. The seat any criminal would naturally point at. It's the seat under the window and for ten years my old friend Tuppy Morgan, bagged it each day at ten. He sat there, reading Horace, and writing to his innumerable aunts, and almost once a year a criminal pointed him out. Oh, Mr Fowle, Tuppy was a limpet on that seat. But this morning, something, possibly a cold, perhaps death, kept him indoors. So I had his place. And you spotted me, no doubt.

FOWLE. Spotted you?

MORGENHALL. My glass polished. My profile drawn and learned in front of the great window.

FOWLE. I never noticed.

MORGENHALL. But when they asked you to choose a lawyer?

FOWLE. I shut my eyes and pointed – I've picked horses that way, and football teams. Never did me any good, though, by any stretch of the imagination.

MORGENHALL. So even you, Mr Fowle, didn't choose me?

FOWLE. Not altogether.

MORGENHALL. The law's a haphazard business.

FOWLE. It does seem chancy.

MORGENHALL. Years of training, and then to be picked out like a football pool.

FOWLE. Don't take it badly sir.

MORGENHALL. Of course, you've been fortunate.

FOWLE. So unusual. I was never one to draw the free bird at Christmas, or guess the weight of the cake. Now I'm sorry I told you.

MORGENHALL. Never mind. You hurt me temporarily, Fowle, I must confess. It might have been kinder to have kept me in ignorance. But now it's done. Let's get down to business. And, Fowle –

FOWLE. Yes, sir.

MORGENHALL. Remember you're dealing with fellow man. A man no longer young. Remember the hopes I've pinned on you and try . . .

FOWLE. Try?

MORGENHALL. Try to spare me more pain.

FOWLE. I will, sir. Of course I will.

MORGENHALL. Now. Let's get our minds in order.

FOWLE. Sort things out?

MORGENHALL. Exactly. Now, this wife of yours.

FOWLE. Doris?

MORGENHALL. Doris. A bitter, unsympathetic woman?

FOWLE. She was always cheerful. She loved jokes.

MORGENHALL. Oh, Fowle. Do be very careful.

FOWLE. I will, sir. But if you'd known Doris. . . . She laughed harder than she worked. 'Thank God,' she'd say, 'for my old English sense of fun.'

MORGENHALL. What sort of jokes, Fowle, did this Doris appreciate?

FOWLE. All sorts. Pictures in the paper. Jokes on the wireless set. Laughs out of crackers, she'd keep them from Christmas to Christmas and trot them out in August.

MORGENHALL. You couldn't share it?

FOWLE. Not to that extent. I often missed the funny point.

MORGENHALL. Then you'd quarrel?

FOWLE. 'Don't look so miserable, it may never happen.' She said that every night when I came home. 'Where'd you get that miserable expression from?'

MORGENHALL. I can see it now. There is a kind of Sunday evening appearance to you.

FOWLE. I was quite happy. But it was always 'Cat got your tongue?' 'Where's the funeral?' 'Play us a tune on that old fiddle face of yours. Lucky there's one of us here that can see the funny side.' Then we had to have our tea with the wireless on, so that she'd pick up the phrases.

MORGENHALL. You're not a wireless lover?

FOWLE. I couldn't always laugh. And she'd be doubled up across the table, gasping as if her lungs were full of water. 'Laugh,' she'd call, 'Laugh, damn you. What've you got to be so miserable about?' Then she'd go under, bubbling like a drowning woman.

MORGENHALL. Made meals difficult?

FOWLE. Indigestible. I would have laughed, but the jokes never tickled me.

MORGENHALL. They tickled her?

FOWLE. Anything did. Anything a little comic. Our names were misfortunate.

MORGENHALL. Your names?

FOWLE. Fowle. Going down the aisle she said: 'Now we're cock and hen, aren't we, old bird?' Coming away, it was 'Now I'm Mrs Fowle, you'll have to play fair with me.' She laughed so hard we couldn't get her straightened up for the photograph.

MORGENHALL. Fond of puns, I gather you're trying to say.

FOWLE. Of any sort of joke. I had a little aviary at the bottom of my garden. As she got funnier so I spent more time with my birds. Budgerigars are small parrots. Circles round their eyes give them a sad, tired look.

MORGENHALL. You found them sympathetic?

FOWLE. Restful. Until one of them spoke out at me.

MORGENHALL. Spoke – what words?

FOWLE. 'Don't look so miserable, it may never happen.'

MORGENHALL. The bird said that?

FOWLE. She taught it during the day when I was out at work. It didn't mean to irritate.

MORGENHALL. It was wrong of her of course. To lead on your bird like that.

FOWLE. But it wasn't him that brought me to it. It was Bateson, the lodger.

MORGENHALL. Another man?

FOWLE. At long last.

MORGENHALL. I can see it now. A crime of passion. An unfaithful wife. *In flagrante* . . . Of course, you don't know what that means. We'll reduce it to manslaughter right away. A wronged husband and there's never a dry eye in the jury-box. You came in and caught them.

FOWLE. Always laughing together.

MORGENHALL. Maddening!

FOWLE. He knew more jokes than she did.

MORGENHALL. Stealing her before your eyes?

FOWLE. That's what I thought. He was a big man. Ex-police. Said he'd been the scream of the station. I picked him for her specially. In the chitty I put up in the local sweet shop, I wrote: 'Humorous type of lodger wanted.'

MORGENHALL. But wasn't that a risk?

FOWLE. Slight, perhaps. But it went all right. Two days after he came he poised a bag of flour to fall on her in the kitchen. Then she sewed up the legs of his pyjamas. They had to hold on to each other so as not to fall over laughing. 'Look at old misery standing there,' she said. 'He can never see anything subtle.'

MORGENHALL. Galling for you. Terribly galling.

FOWLE. I thought all was well. I spent more time with the

birds. I'd come home late and always be careful to scrunch the gravel at the front door. I went to bed early and left them with the Light Programme. On Sunday mornings I fed the budgies and suggested he took her tea in bed. 'Laughter,' she read out from her horoscope, 'leads to love, even for those born under the sign of the Virgin.'

MORGENHALL. You trusted them. They deceived you.

FOWLE. They deceived me all right. And I trusted them. Especially after I'd seen her on his knee and them both looking at the cartoons from one wrapping of chips.

MORGENHALL. Mr Fowle. I'm not quite getting the drift of your evidence. My hope is – your thought may not prove a shade too involved for our literal-minded judge. Old Tommy Banter was a Rugger blue in '98. He never rose to chess and his draughts had a brutal, unintelligent quality.

FOWLE. When he'd first put his knee under her I thought he'd do the decent thing. I thought I'd have peace in my little house at last. The wireless set dead silent. The end of all the happy laughter. No sound but the twitter from the end of the garden and the squeak of my own foot on the linoleum.

MORGENHALL. You wanted . . .

FOWLE. I heard them whispering together and my hopes raised high. Then I came back and he was gone.

MORGENHALL. She'd . . .

FOWLE. Turned him out. Because he was getting over familiar. 'I couldn't have that.' she said. 'I may like my laugh, but thank God, I'm still respectable. No thank you, there's safety in marriage. So I'm stuck with you, fiddle face. Let's play a tune on it, shall we?' She'd sent him away, my last hope.

MORGENHALL. So you . . .

FOWLE. I realize I did wrong.

MORGENHALL. You could have left.

FOWLE. Who'd have fed the birds? That thought was upper-most.

MORGENHALL. So it's not a crime of passion?

FOWLE. Not if you put it like that.

MORGENHALL. Mr Fowle. I've worked and waited for you. Now, you're the only case I've got, *and* the most difficult.

FOWLE. I'm sorry.

MORGENHALL. A man could crack his head against a case like you and still be far from a solution. Can't you see how twelve honest hearts will snap like steel when they learn you ended up your wife because she *wouldn't* leave you?

FOWLE. If she had left, there wouldn't have been the need.

MORGENHALL. There's no doubt about it. As I look at you now, I see you're an unsympathetic figure.

FOWLE. There it is.

MORGENHALL. It'll need a brilliant stroke to save you. An unexpected move – something pulled out of a hat – I've got it. Something really exciting. The surprise witness.

FOWLE. Witness?

MORGENHALL. Picture the scene, Mr Fowle. The Court room silent. The jury about to sink you. The prosecution flushed with victory. And then I rise, my voice a hoarse whisper, exhausted by that long trial. 'My Lord. If your Lordship pleases.'

FOWLE. What are you saying?

MORGENHALL. Do you expect me to do this off the cuff, Fowle, with no sort of rehearsal?

FOWLE. No. . . .

MORGENHALL. Take the stool and co-operate, man. Now, that towel over your head, please, to simulate the dirty grey wig – already you appear anonymous and vaguely alarming.

MORGENHALL *arranges* FOWLE *on the stool. Drapes the towel over his head.*

Now, my dear Fowle, forget your personality. You're Sir

Tommy Banter, living with a widowed sister in a draughty great morgue on Wimbledon Common. Digestion, bad. Politics, an Independent Moral Conservative. Favourite author, doesn't read. Diversions, snooker in the basement of the morgue, peeping at the lovers on the Common and money being given away on the television. In love with capital punishment, corporal punishment, and a younger brother who is accomplished at embroidery. A small, alarmed man, frightened of the great dog he lives with to give him the air of a country squire. Served with distinction in the Great War at sentencing soldiers to long terms of imprisonment. A man without friends, unexpectedly adored by a great-niece, three years old.

FOWLE. I am?

MORGENHALL. Him.

FOWLE. It feels strange.

MORGENHALL. Now, my Lord. I ask your Lordship's leave to call the surprise witness.

FOWLE. Certainly.

MORGENHALL. What?

FOWLE. Certainly.

MORGENHALL. For Heaven's sake, Fowle, this is like practising bull-fights with a kitten. Here's an irregular application by the defence, something that might twist the trial in the prisoner's favour and prevent you catching the connection at Charing Cross. Your breakfast's like a lead weight on your chest. Your sister, plunging at Spot last night, ripped the cloth. The dog bit your ankle on the way downstairs. No, blind yourself with rage and terrible justice.

FOWLE. No. You can't call the surprise witness.

MORGENHALL. That's better. Oh, my Lord. If your Lordship would listen to me.

FOWLE. Certainly not. You've had your chance. Let's get on with it.

MORGENHALL. My Lord. Justice must not only be done, but

must clearly be seen to be done. No one knows, as yet, what my surprise witness will say. Perhaps he'll say the prisoner is guilty in his black heart as your Lordship thinks. But perhaps, gentlemen of the jury, we have trapped an innocent. If so, shall we deny him the one door through which he might walk to freedom? The public outcry would never die down.

FOWLE (*snatching off the towel and rising angrily to his feet*). Hear, hear!

MORGENHALL. What's that?

FOWLE. The public outcry.

MORGENHALL. Excellent. Now, towel back on. You're the judge.

FOWLE (*as the Judge*). Silence! I'll have all those noisy people put out. Very well. Call the witness. But keep it short.

MORGENHALL. Wonderful. Very good. Now. Deathly silence as the witness walks through the breathless crowds. Let's see the surprise witness. Take the towel off.

FOWLE (*moves from the stool and, standing very straight says*): I swear to tell the truth . . .

MORGENHALL. You've got a real feeling for the Law. A pity you came to it so late in life.

FOWLE. The whole truth.

MORGENHALL. Now, what's your name?

FOWLE (*absent minded*). Herbert Fowle.

MORGENHALL. No, no. You're the witness.

FOWLE. Martin Jones.

MORGENHALL. Excellent. Now, you know Herbert Fowle?

FOWLE. All my life.

MORGENHALL. Always found him respectable?

FOWLE. Very quiet spoken man, and clean living.

MORGENHALL. Where was he when this crime took place?

FOWLE. He was . . .

MORGENHALL. Just a moment. My Lord, will you sharpen a pencil and note this down?

FOWLE. You'd dare to say that? To him?

MORGENHALL. Fearlessness, Mr Fowle. The first essential in an advocate. Is your Lordship's pencil poised?

FOWLE (as Judge). Yes, yes. Get on with it.

MORGENHALL. Where was he?

FOWLE (as Witness). In my house.

MORGENHALL. All the evening?

FOWLE. Playing whist. I went to collect him and we left Mrs Fowle well and happy. I returned with him and she'd been removed to the Country and General.

MORGENHALL. Panic stirs the prosecution benches. The prosecutor tries a few fumbling questions. But you stand your ground, don't you?

FOWLE. Certainly.

MORGENHALL. My Lord. I demand the prisoner be released.

FOWLE (as Judge). Certainly. Can't think what all this fuss has been about. Release the prisoner, and reduce all police officers in Court to the rank of P.C.

Pause.

MORGENHALL. Fowle.

FOWLE. Yes, sir.

MORGENHALL. Aren't you going to thank me?

FOWLE. I don't know what I can say.

MORGENHALL. Words don't come easily to you, do they?

FOWLE. Very hard.

MORGENHALL. You could just stand and stammer in a touching way and offer me that old gold watch of your father's.

FOWLE. But . . .

MORGENHALL. Well, I think we've pulled your chestnuts out of the fire. We'll just have to make sure of this fellow Jones.

FOWLE. But . . .

MORGENHALL. Fowle, you're a good simple chap, but there's no need to interrupt my thinking.

FOWLE. I was only reminding you . . .

MORGENHALL. Well, what?

FOWLE. We have no Jones.

MORGENHALL. Carried off in a cold spell? Then we can get his statement in under the Evidence Act.

FOWLE. He never lived. We made him up.

Pause.

MORGENHALL. Fowle.

FOWLE. Yes, sir.

MORGENHALL. It's remarkable a thing, but with no legal training, I think you've put your finger on a fatal weakness in our defence.

FOWLE. I was afraid it might be so.

MORGENHALL. It is so.

FOWLE. Then we'd better just give in.

MORGENHALL. Give in? We do not give in. When my life depends on this case.

FOWLE. I forgot. Then, we must try.

MORGENHALL. Yes. Brain! Brain! Go to work. It'll come to me, you know, in an illuminating flash. Hard relentless brain work. This is the way I go at the crosswords and I never give up. I have it. Bateson!

FOWLE. The lodger?

MORGENHALL. Bateson, the lodger. I never liked him. Under a ruthless cross-examination, you know, he might confess that it was he. Do you see a flash?

FOWLE. You look much happier.

MORGENHALL. I am much happier. And when I begin my ruthless cross-examination. . . .

FOWLE. Would you care to try it?

MORGENHALL. Mr Fowle. You and I are learning to muck in splendidly together over this. Mr Bateson.

FOWLE (*as Bateson, lounging in an imaginary witness box with his hands in his pockets*). Yes. Sir?

MORGENHALL. Perhaps, when you address the Court you'd be good enough to take your hands out of your pockets. Not you Mr Fowle, of course. You became on very friendly terms with the prisoner's wife?

FOWLE. We had one or two good old laughs together.

MORGENHALL. Was the association entirely innocent?

FOWLE. Innocent laughs. Jokes without offence. The cracker or Christmas card variety. No jokes that would have shamed a postcard.

MORGENHALL. And to tell those innocent jokes, did you have to sit very close to Mrs Fowle?

FOWLE. How do you mean?

MORGENHALL. Did you have to sit beneath her?

FOWLE. I don't understand.

MORGENHALL. Did she perch upon your knee?

FOWLE (*horrified intake of breath*).

MORGENHALL. What was that?

FOWLE. Shocked breathing from the jury, sir.

MORGENHALL. Having its effect, eh? Now, Mr Bateson. Will you kindly answer my question.

FOWLE. You're trying to trap me.

MORGENHALL. Not trying, Bateson, succeeding.

FOWLE. Well, she may have rested on my knee. Once or twice.

MORGENHALL. And you loved her, guiltily?

FOWLE. I may have done.

MORGENHALL. And planned to take her away with you?

FOWLE. I did ask her.

MORGENHALL. And when she refused. . . .

FOWLE (*as Judge*). Just a moment. Where's all this leading?

MORGENHALL. Your Lordship asks me! My Lord, it is our case that it was this man, Bateson, enraged by the refusal of the prisoner's wife to follow him, who struck . . . You see where we've got to?

FOWLE. I do.

MORGENHALL. Masterly. I think you'll have to agree with me?

FOWLE. Of course.

MORGENHALL. No flaws in this one?

FOWLE. Not really a flaw, sir. Perhaps a little hitch.

MORGENHALL. A hitch. Go on. Break it down.

FOWLE. No, sir, really. Not after you've been so kind.

MORGENHALL. Never mind. All my life I've stood against the winds of criticism and neglect. My gown may be a little tattered, my cuffs frayed. There may be a hole in my sock for the draughts to get at me. Quite often, on my way to Court, I notice that my left shoe lets in water. I am used to hardship. Speak on, Mr Fowle.

FOWLE. Soon as he left my house, Bateson was stopped by an officer. He'd lifted an alarm clock off me, and the remains of a bottle of port. They booked him straight away.

MORGENHALL. You mean, there wasn't time?

FOWLE. Hardly. Two hours later the next door observed Mrs Fowle at the washing. Then I came home.

MORGENHALL. Fowle. Do you want to help me?

FOWLE. Of course. Haven't I shown it?

MORGENHALL. But you will go on putting all these difficulties in my way.

FOWLE. I knew you'd be upset.

MORGENHALL. Not really. After all, I'm a grown up, even an old, man. At my age one expects little gratitude. There's a cat I feed each day at my lodgings, a waitress in the lunch room here who always gets that sixpence under my plate. In ten, twenty years' time, will they remember me? Oh, I'm not bitter. But a little help, just a very little encouragement. . . .

FOWLE. But you'll win this case. A brilliant mind like yours.

MORGENHALL. Yes. Thank God. It's very brilliant.

FOWLE. And all that training.

MORGENHALL. Years of it. Hard, hard training.

FOWLE. You'll solve it, sir.

Pause.

MORGENHALL. Fowle. Do you know what I've heard Tuppy Morgan say? After all, he's sat here, year in, year out, as long as anyone can remember, in Court, waiting for the Dock Brief himself. Wilfred, he's frequently told me, if they ever give you a brief, old fellow, attack the medical evidence. Remember, the jury's full of rheumatism and arthritis and shocking gastric troubles. They love to see a medical man put through it. Always go for a doctor.

FOWLE (eagerly). You'd like to try?

MORGENHALL. Shall we?

FOWLE. I'd enjoy it.

MORGENHALL. Doctor. Did you say the lady died of heart failure?

FOWLE (as Doctor). No.

MORGENHALL. Come, Doctor. Don't fence with me. Her heart wasn't normal when you examined her, was it?

FOWLE. She was dead.

MORGENHALL. So it had stopped.

FOWLE. Yes.

MORGENHALL. Then her heart had failed?

FOWLE. Well . . .

MORGENHALL. So she died of heart failure?

FOWLE. But . . .

MORGENHALL. And heart failure might have been brought on by a fit, I say a fit of laughter, at a curiously rich joke on the wireless?

FOWLE. Whew!

FOWLE claps softly. Pause.

MORGENHALL. Thank you, Fowle. It was kind but, I thought,

hollow. I don't believe my attack on the doctor was convincing.

FOWLE. Perhaps a bit unlikely. But clever. . . .

MORGENHALL. Too clever. No. We're not going to win this on science, Fowle. Science must be thrown away. As I asked those questions, I saw I wasn't even convincing you of your own innocence. But you respond to emotion, Fowle, as I do, the magic of oratory, the wonderful power of words.

FOWLE. Now you're talking.

MORGENHALL. I'm going to talk.

FOWLE. I wish I could hear some of it. Words as grand as print.

MORGENHALL. A golden tongue. A voice like a lyre to charm you out of hell.

FOWLE. Now you've commenced to wander away from all I've understood.

MORGENHALL. I was drawing on the riches of my classical education which comforts me on buses, waiting at surgeries, or in prison cells. But I shall speak to the jury simply, without classical allusions. I shall say . . .

FOWLE. Yes.

MORGENHALL. I shall say . . .

FOWLE. What?

MORGENHALL. I had it on the tip of my tongue.

FOWLE. Oh.

MORGENHALL. I shan't disappoint you. I shall speak for a day, perhaps two days. At the end I shall say . . .

FOWLE. Yes? Just the closing words.

MORGENHALL. The closing words.

FOWLE. To clinch the argument.

MORGENHALL. Yes. The final, irrefutable argument.

FOWLE. If I could only hear.

MORGENHALL. You shall, Fowle. You shall hear it. In Court. It'll come out in Court, and when I sink back in my seat, trembling, and wipe the real tears off my glasses. . . .

FOWLE. The judge's summing up.

MORGENHALL. What will Tommy say?

FOWLE (*as Judge*). Members of the jury . . .

MORGENHALL. Struggling with emotions as well.

FOWLE. I can't add anything to the words of the barrister. Go out and consider your verdict.

MORGENHALL. Have they left the box?

FOWLE. Only a formality.

MORGENHALL. I see. I wonder how long they'll be out.

Pause.

They're out a long time.

FOWLE. Of course, it must seem long to you. The suspense.

MORGENHALL. I hope they won't disagree.

FOWLE. I don't see how they can.

Pause.

MORGENHALL. Fowle.

FOWLE. Yes, sir.

MORGENHALL. Shall we just take a peep into the jury room.

FOWLE. I wish we could.

MORGENHALL. Let's. Let me see, you're the foreman?

FOWLE. I take it we're all agreed, chaps. So let's sit here and have a short smoke.

They sit on the bench together.

MORGENHALL. An excellent idea. The barrister saved him.

FOWLE. That wonderful speech. I had a bit of doubt before I heard the speech.

MORGENHALL. No doubt now, have you?

FOWLE. Certainly not.

They light imaginary pipes.

Care for a fill of mine?

MORGENHALL. Thank you so much. Match?

FOWLE. Here you are.

MORGENHALL. I say, you don't think the poor fellow's in any doubt, do you?

FOWLE. No. He must know he'll get off. After the speech I mean.

MORGENHALL. I mean, I wouldn't like him to be on pins. . . .

FOWLE. Think we ought to go back and reassure him?

They move off the bench.

MORGENHALL. As you wish. Careful that pipe doesn't start a fire in your pocket. (*As Clerk of Court*). Gentlemen of the jury. Have you considered your verdict?

FOWLE. We have.

MORGENHALL. And do you find the prisoner guilty or not guilty?

FOWLE. Not guilty, my Lord.

MORGENHALL. Hooray!

FOWLE (*as Judge*). Now, if there's any sort of Mafeking around, I'll have the Court closed.

MORGENHALL. So I'm surrounded, mobbed. Tuppy Morgan wrings my hand and says it was lucky he left the seat. The judge sends me a letter of congratulation. The journalists dart off to their little telephones. And what now: 'Of course they'd make you a judge but you're probably too busy. . . .' There's a queue of solicitors on the stairs. . . . My old clerk writes on my next brief, a thousand guineas to divorce a duchess. There are questions of new clothes, laying down the port. Oh, Mr Fowle, the change in life you've brought me.

FOWLE. It will be your greatest day.

MORGENHALL. Yes, Mr Fowle. My greatest day.

The bolts shoot back, the door opens slowly.

What's that? I said we weren't to be interrupted. It's

draughty in here with that door open. Close it, there's a good chap, do.

FOWLE. I think, you know, they must want us for the trial. FOWLE *goes through the door.* MORGENHALL *follows with a dramatic sweep of his gown.*

The Curtain Falls

Scene Two

When the curtain rises again the sky through the windows shows that it is late afternoon. The door is unlocked and MORGENHALL *enters. He is without his wig and gown, more agitated than ever, he speaks to the* WARDER, *off stage.*

MORGENHALL. He's not here at the moment – he's not . . . ? Oh, I'm so glad. Just out temporarily? With the governor? Then, I'll wait for him. Poor soul. How's he taking it? You're not allowed to answer questions? The regulations, I suppose. Well, you must obey the regulations. I'll just sit down here and wait for Mr Fowle.

The door closes.

(*He whistles. Whistling stops.*) May it please you, my Lord, members of the jury. I should have said, may it please you, my *Lord*, members of the jury. I should have said . . .

He begins to walk up and down.

Members of the jury. Is there one of you who doesn't crave for peace . . . crave for peace. The silence of an undisturbed life, the dignity of an existence without dependants . . . without jokes. Have you never been tempted?
I should have said . . .
Members of the *jury*. You and I are men of the world. If your Lordship would kindly not interrupt my speech to the jury. I'm obliged. Members of the jury, before I was so rudely interrupted.
I might have said . . .
Look at the prisoner, members of the jury. Has he hurt you, done you the slightest harm? Is he not the mildest of men?

He merely took it upon himself to regulate his domestic affairs. An Englishman's home is his castle. Do any of you feel a primitive urge, members of the jury, to be revenged on this gentle bird fancier. . . .

Members of the jury, I see I'm affecting your emotions but let us consider the weight of the evidence . . . I might have said that!

I might have said . . . (*with distress*) I might have said something. . . .

The door opens. FOWLE *enters. He is smiling to himself, but as soon as he sees* MORGENHALL *he looks serious and solicitous.*

FOWLE. I was hoping you'd find time to drop in, sir. I'm afraid you're upset.

MORGENHALL. No, no, my dear chap. Not at all upset.

FOWLE. The result of the trial's upset you.

MORGENHALL. I feel a little dashed. A little out of sorts.

FOWLE. It was disappointing for you.

MORGENHALL. A touch of disappointment. But there'll be other cases. There may be other cases.

FOWLE. But you'd built such high hopes on this particular one.

MORGENHALL. Well, there it is, Fowle.

FOWLE. It doesn't do to expect too much of a particular thing.

MORGENHALL. You're right, of course.

FOWLE. Year after year I used to look forward keenly to the Feathered Friends Fanciers' Annual Do. Invariably it took the form of a dinner.

MORGENHALL. Your yearly treat?

FOWLE. Exactly. All I had in the enjoyment line. Each year I built high hopes on it. June 13th, I'd say, now there's an evening to look forward to.

MORGENHALL. Something to live for?

FOWLE. In a way. But when it came, you know, it was never up to it. Your collar was always too tight, or the food was inadequate, or someone had a nasty scene with the fancier in the chair. So, on June 14th, I always said to myself: Thank God for a night at home.

MORGENHALL. It came and went and your life didn't change?

FOWLE. No, quite frankly.

MORGENHALL. And this case has left me just as I was before.

FOWLE. Don't say that.

MORGENHALL. Tuppy Morgan's back in his old seat under the window. The judge never congratulated me. No one's rung up to offer me a brief. I thought my old clerk looked coldly at me, and there was a titter in the luncheon room when I ordered my usual roll and tomato soup.

FOWLE. But I . . .

MORGENHALL. And you're not left in a very favourable position.

FOWLE. Don't say that, sir. It's not so bad for me. After all, I had no education.

MORGENHALL. So many years before I could master the Roman Law relating to the ownership of chariots. . . .

FOWLE. Wasted, you think?

MORGENHALL. I feel so.

FOWLE. But without that rich background, would an individual have been able to sway the Court as you did?

MORGENHALL. Sway?

FOWLE. The Court.

MORGENHALL. Did I do that?

FOWLE. It struck me you did.

MORGENHALL. Indeed. . . .

FOWLE. It's turned out masterly.

MORGENHALL. Mr Fowle, you're trying to be kind. When I was a child I played French cricket with an uncle who deliberately allowed the ball to strike his legs. At the age of seven that irked me. At sixty-three I can face the difficulties of accurate batting. . . .

FOWLE. But no, sir. I really mean it. I owe it all to you. Where I am.

MORGENHALL. I'm afraid near the end.

FOWLE. Just commencing.

MORGENHALL. I lost, Mr Fowle. You may not be aware of it. It may not have been hammered home to you yet. But your case is lost.

FOWLE. But there are ways and ways of losing.

MORGENHALL. That's true, of course.

FOWLE. I noticed your artfulness right at the start, when the policeman gave evidence. You pulled out that red handkerchief, slowly and deliberately, like a conjuring trick.

MORGENHALL. And blew?

FOWLE. A sad, terrible trumpet.

MORGENHALL. Unnerved him, I thought.

FOWLE. He never recovered. There was no call to ask questions after that.

MORGENHALL. And then they called that doctor.

FOWLE. You were right not to bother with him.

MORGENHALL. Tactics, you see. We'd decided not to trouble with science.

FOWLE. So we had. And with Bateson . . .

MORGENHALL. No, Fowle. I must beware of your flattery, I think I might have asked Bateson . . .

FOWLE. It wouldn't have made a farthing's difference. A glance told them he was a demon.

MORGENHALL. He stood there, so big and red, with his no tie and dirty collar. I rose up to question him and suddenly it seemed as if there were no reason for us to converse. I remembered what you said about his jokes, his familiarity with your wife. What had he and I in common? I turned from him in disgust. I think that jury guessed the reason for my silence with friend Bateson.

FOWLE. I think they did!

MORGENHALL. But when it came to the speech. . . .

FOWLE. The best stroke of all.

MORGENHALL. I can't agree. You no longer carry me with you.

FOWLE. Said from the heart.

MORGENHALL. I'm sure of it. But not, dare I say, altogether justified? We can't pretend, can we, Mr Fowle, that the speech was a success?

FOWLE. It won the day.

MORGENHALL. I beg you not to be under any illusions. They found you guilty.

FOWLE. I was forgetting. But that masterly speech. . . .

MORGENHALL. I can't be hoodwinked.

FOWLE. But you don't know. . . .

MORGENHALL. I stood up, Mr Fowle, and it was the moment I'd waited for. Ambition had driven me to it, the moment when I was alone with what I wanted. Everyone turned to me, twelve blank faces in the jury box, eager to have the grumpy looks wiped off them. The judge was silent. The prosecutor courteously pretended to be asleep. I only had to open my mouth and pour words out. What stopped me?

FOWLE. What?

MORGENHALL. Fear. That's what's suggested. That's what the clerks tittered to the waitress in Friday's luncheon room. Old Wilf Morgenhall was in a funk.

FOWLE. More shame on them. . . .

MORGENHALL. But it wasn't so. Nor did my mind go blank. When I rose I knew exactly what I was going to say.

FOWLE. Then, why?

MORGENHALL. Not say it – you were going to say?

FOWLE. It had struck me –

MORGENHALL. It must have, Fowle. It must have struck many people. You'll forgive a reminiscence. . . .

FOWLE. Glad of one.

MORGENHALL. The lady I happened to mention yesterday. I don't of course, often speak of her. . . .

FOWLE. She, who, in the 1914 . . . ?

MORGENHALL. Exactly. But I lost her long before that. For years, you know, Mr Fowle, this particular lady and I met at tea parties, tennis, and so on. Then, one evening, I walked home with her. We stood on Vauxhall Bridge, a warm Summer night, and silence fell. It was the moment when I should have spoken, the obvious moment. Then, something overcame me, it wasn't shyness or fear then, but a tremendous exhaustion. I was tired out by the long wait, and when the opportunity came – all I could think of was sleep.

FOWLE. It's a relief. . . .

MORGENHALL. To go home alone. To undress, clean your teeth, knock out your pipe, not to bother with failure or success.

FOWLE. So yesterday . . .

MORGENHALL. I had lived through that moment so many times. It happened every day in my mind, daydreaming on buses, or in the doctor's surgery. When it came, I was tired of it. The exhaustion came over me. I wanted it to be all over. I wanted to be alone in my room, in the darkness, with a soft pillow round my ears. . . . So I failed.

FOWLE. Don't say it.

MORGENHALL. Being too tired to make my daydream public. It's a nice day. Summer's coming.

FOWLE. No, don't sir. Not too near the window.

MORGENHALL. Why not, Mr Fowle?

FOWLE. I was concerned. A man in your position might be desperate. . . .

MORGENHALL. You say you can see the forest?

FOWLE. Just a glimpse of it.

MORGENHALL. I think I shall retire from the bar.

FOWLE. Don't say it, sir. After that rigorous training.

MORGENHALL. Well, there it is. I think I shall retire.

FOWLE. But cheer up, sir. As you said, other cases, other days. Let's take this calmly, sir. Let's be very lucid, as you put it in your own statement.

MORGENHALL. Other cases? I'm getting on, you know. Tuppy Morgan's back in his place. I doubt if the Dock Brief will come round again.

FOWLE. But there'll be something.

MORGENHALL. What can there be? Unless?

FOWLE. Yes, sir?

MORGENHALL. There would be another brief if . . .

FOWLE. Yes?

MORGENHALL. I advised you to appeal. . . .

FOWLE. Ah, now that, misfortunately . . .

MORGENHALL. There's a different atmosphere there, up in the Appeal Court, Fowle. It's far from the rough and tumble, question and answer, swear on the Bible and lie your way out of it. It's quiet up there. Pure Law, of course. Yes. I believe I'm cut out for the Court of Appeal. . . .

FOWLE. But you see . . .

MORGENHALL. A big, quiet Court in the early Summer afternoon. Piles of books, and when you put one down the dust and powdered leather rises and makes the ushers sneeze. The clock ticks. Three old judges in scarlet take snuff with trembling hands. You'll sit in the dock and not follow a legal word. And I'll give them all my Law and get you off on a technicality.

FOWLE. But today . . .

MORGENHALL. Now, if I may remind your Lordships of Prickle against the Haverfordwest Justice *ex parte* Anger, reported in 96 Moor's Ecclesiastical at page a thousand and three. Have your Lordships the report? Lord Bradwell, C. J., says, at the foot of the page: 'The guilty intention is a deep foundation stone in the wall of our jurisprudence. So if it be that Prickle did run the bailiff through with his poignard taking him for a stray dog or cat, it seems there would be well raised the plea of autrefois mistake. But, contra, if he thought him to be his neighbour's cat, then, as my Brother Breadwinkle has well said in Lord Roche and Anderson, there might fall out a constructive larceny and felo in rem.' Oh, Mr Fowle, I have some of these fine cases by heart.

FOWLE. Above me, I'm afraid, you're going now.

MORGENHALL. Of course I am. These cases always bore the prisoner until they're upheld or overruled and he comes out dead or alive at the end of it all.

FOWLE. I'd like to hear you reading them, though. . . .

MORGENHALL. You will. I'll be followed to Court by my clerk, an old tortoise burdened by the weight of authorities. Then he'll lay them out in a fine buff and half calf row, a letter from a clergyman I correspond with in Wales torn to mark each place. A glass of water, a dry cough and the 'My respectful submission'.

FOWLE. And that, of course, is . . .

MORGENHALL. That the judge misdirected himself. He forgot the rule in Rimmer's case, he confused his *mens sana,* he displaced the burden of proof, he played fast and loose with all reasonable doubt, he kicked the presumption of innocence round like a football.

FOWLE. Strong words.

MORGENHALL. I shan't let Tommy Banter off lightly.

FOWLE. The judge?

MORGENHALL. Thoroughly unscholarly. Not a word of Latin in the whole summing up.

FOWLE. Not up to you, of course.

MORGENHALL. Thank God, I kept my books. There have been times, Fowle, when I was tempted, pricked and harried for rent perhaps, to have my clerk barter the whole lot away for the few pounds they offer for centuries of entombed law.

But I stuck to them. I still have my Swabey and Tristram, my Pod's *Privy Council*, my Spinks' *Prize Cases*. I shall open them up and say . . . I shall say . . .

FOWLE. It's no good.

MORGENHALL. What's no good?

FOWLE. It's no good appealing.

MORGENHALL. No good?

FOWLE. No good at all.

MORGENHALL. Mr Fowle. I've worked hard for you.

FOWLE. True enough.

MORGENHALL. And I mean to go on working.

FOWLE. It's a great comfort . . .

MORGENHALL. In the course of our close, and may I say it? yes, our happy collaboration on this little crime of yours, I've become almost fond of you.

FOWLE. Thank you, sir.

MORGENHALL. At first, I have to admit it, I was put off by your somewhat furtive and repulsive appearance. I saw, I quite agree, only the outer husk, and what I saw was a small man marked by all the physical signs of confirmed criminality.

FOWLE. No oil painting?

MORGENHALL. Let's agree on that at once.

FOWLE. The wife thought so, too.

MORGENHALL. Enough of her, poor woman.

FOWLE. Oh, agreed.

MORGENHALL. My first solicitude for your well-being, let's face up to this as well, had a selfish element. You were my very own case, and I didn't want to lose you.

FOWLE. Natural feelings. But still . . .

MORGENHALL. I haven't wounded you?

FOWLE. Nothing fatal.

MORGENHALL. I'm glad. Because, you know, as we worked on this case together, an affection sprang up . . .

FOWLE. Mutual.

MORGENHALL. You seemed to have a real desire to help, and, if I may say so, an instinctive taste for the law.

FOWLE. A man can't go through this sort of thing without getting legal interests.

MORGENHALL. Quite so. And of course, as a self-made man, that's to your credit. But I did notice, just at the start, some flaws in you as a client.

FOWLE. Flaws?

MORGENHALL. You may not care to admit it. But let's be honest. After all, we don't want to look on the dreary side; but you may not be with us for very long. . . .

FOWLE. That's what I was trying to say. . . .

MORGENHALL. Please, Mr Fowle, no interruptions until we've cleared this out of the way. Now didn't you, just at the beginning, put unnecessary difficulties before us?

FOWLE. Did I?

MORGENHALL. I well remember, before I got a bit of keenness into you, that you seemed about to admit your guilt.

FOWLE. Oh. . . .

MORGENHALL. Just a little obstinate, wasn't it?

FOWLE. I dare say. . . .

MORGENHALL. And now, when I've worked for fifty years to get the Law at my finger-tips, I hear you mutter, 'No appeal'.

FOWLE. No appeal!

MORGENHALL. Mr Fowle. . . .

FOWLE. Yesterday you asked me to spare you pain, sir. This is going to be very hard for me.

MORGENHALL. What?

FOWLE. As you say, we've worked together, and I've had the pleasure of watching the ticking over of a legal mind. If you'd call any afternoon I'd be pleased to repay the compliment by showing you my birds. . . .

MORGENHALL. Not in this world you must realize, unless we appeal.

FOWLE. You see, this morning I saw the Governor.

MORGENHALL. You had some complaint?

FOWLE. I don't want to boast, but the truth is . . . he sent for me.

MORGENHALL. You went in fear . . .

FOWLE. And trembling. But he turned out a very gentlemanly sort of individual. Ex-Army, I should imagine. All the ornaments of a gentleman. Wife and children in a tinted photo framed on the desk, handsome oil painting of a prize pig over the mantelpiece. Healthy red face. Strong smell of scented soap. . . .

MORGENHALL. But grow to the point. . . .

FOWLE. I'm telling you. 'Well, Fowle' he says, 'Sit down do. I'm just finishing this letter.' So I sat and looked out of his windows. Big wide windows in the Governor's office, and the view. . . .

MORGENHALL. Fowle. If this anecdote has any point, be a good little chap, reach it.

FOWLE. Of course it has, where was I?

MORGENHALL. Admiring the view as usual.

FOWLE. Panoramic it was. Well, this Governor individual, finishing his letter, lit up one of those flat type of Egyptian cigarettes. 'Well, Fowle,' he said . . .

MORGENHALL. Yes, yes. It's not necessary, Fowle, to reproduce every word of this conversation. Give us the gist, just the meat, you understand. Leave out the trimmings.

FOWLE. Trimmings there weren't. He put it quite bluntly.

MORGENHALL. What did he put?

FOWLE. 'Well, Fowle, this may surprise you. But the Home Office was on the telephone about you this morning.' Isn't that a Government department?

MORGENHALL. Yes, yes, and well . . .

FOWLE. It seems they do, in his words, come through from time to time, and just on business, of course, on that blower. And quite frankly, he admitted he was as shocked as I was. But the drill is, as he phrased it, a reprieve.

MORGENHALL. A . . . ?

FOWLE. It's all over. I'm free. It seems that trial was no good at all. . . .

MORGENHALL. No good. But why?

FOWLE. Oh, no particular reason.

MORGENHALL. There must be a reason. Nothing passes in the Law without a reason.

FOWLE. You won't care to know.

MORGENHALL. Tell me.

FOWLE. You're too busy to wait. . . .

MORGENHALL. Tell me, Mr Fowle. I beg of you. Tell me directly why this Governor, who knows nothing of the Law, should have called our one and only trial together 'No good'.

FOWLE. You yourself taught me not to scatter information like bombs.

MORGENHALL. Mr Fowle. You must answer my question. My legal career may depend on it. If I'm not to have wasted my life on useless trials.

FOWLE. You want to hear?

MORGENHALL. Certainly.

FOWLE. He may not have been serious. There was a twinkle, most likely, in his eye.

MORGENHALL. But he said . . .

FOWLE. That the barrister they chose for me was no good. An old crock, in his words. No good at all. That he never said a word in my defence. So my case never got to the jury. He said the whole business was ever so null and void, but I'd better be careful in the future. . . .

MORGENHALL *runs across the cell, mounts the stool, begins to undo his tie.*

No! Mr Morgenhall! Come down from there! No, sir! Don't do it.

They struggle. FOWLE *brings Morgenhall to earth.*

Don't you see? If I'd had a barrister who asked questions,

and made clever speeches I'd be as dead as mutton. Your artfulness saved me. . . .

MORGENHALL. My . . .

FOWLE. The artful way you handled it. The dumb tactics. They paid off! I'm alive!

MORGENHALL. There is that. . . .

FOWLE. And so are you.

MORGENHALL. We both are?

FOWLE. I'm free.

MORGENHALL. To go back to your birds. I suppose . . .

FOWLE. Yes, Mr Morgenhall?

MORGENHALL. It's unlikely you'll marry again?

FOWLE. Unlikely.

Long pause.

MORGENHALL. But you have the clear appearance of a criminal. I suppose it's not impossible that you might commit some rather more trivial offence.

FOWLE. A man can't live, Mr Morgenhall, without committing some trivial offences. Almost daily.

MORGENHALL. Then we may meet again. You may need my services. . . .

FOWLE. Constantly.

MORGENHALL. The future may not be so black. . . .

FOWLE. The sun's shining.

MORGENHALL. Can we go?

FOWLE. I think the door's been open some time. (*He tries it. It is unbolted and swings open.*) After you, Mr Morgenhall, please.

MORGENHALL. No, no.

FOWLE. A man of your education should go first.

MORGENHALL. I think you should lead the way, Mr Fowle, and as your legal adviser I will follow at a discreet distance, to straighten out such little tangles as you may hope to leave in your wake. Let's go.

MORGENHALL: *whistles his fragment of tune.* FOWLE: *his whistle joins* MORGENHALL'S. *Whistling they leave the cell,* MORGENHALL *executing, as he leaves, the steps of a small delighted dance.*

Slow Curtain

What Shall We Tell Caroline?

Michael Codron with David Hall (for Talbot Productions Ltd.) presented *What Shall We Tell Caroline?*
in a double bill (with *The Dock Brief*) at the Lyric
Opera House, Hammersmith, on April 9, 1958, and
on May 20, 1958 at the Garrick Theatre. The cast
was as follows:

LILY LOUDON ('BIN')	*Brenda Bruce*
ARTHUR LOUDON	*Maurice Denham*
TONY PETERS	*Michael Hordern*
CAROLINE	*Marianne Benet*

Directed by Stuart Burge
Designed by Disley Jones

Scene One

The LOUDON'S *living room at 'Highland Close School', Coldsands.
It is an extremely dilapidated room given an air of festivity, as
the curtain rises, by the fact that a table is set for four and there
are candles in odd candlesticks – one expensive silver, the other a
china 'Present from Coldsands' on the table. Doors on each side of
the room, one, left, is covered in green baize and has pinned on it a
few yellowing curling notices and charts of lessons which haven't
been read for years. The door is closed and leads to the boys' part
of the house. The door on the right is open and light floods through
it from a staircase which leads to the bedrooms. Another door
backstage right leads to the kitchen. At the back of the room tall
French windows, which have never shut properly and let in winds
of icy severity, open on to a strip of grey asphalt, the white end
of a flag pole and the gun-metal sky of an early evening in March.*

*Other furniture : a basket-work chair, a fireplace full of paper,
a very small electric fire, a horse-hair sofa wounded and bleeding
its stuffing ; a roll top desk out of which bills, writs, exercise books
and reports are perpetually being shaken by the draughts like the
leaves of a dead tree. On top of the desk there is a ukelele and a
globe. Among faded photographs of various teams an oar is
hanging on the wall.*

As the curtain rises LILY LOUDON *has her back to the
audience and is tugging at one of the drawers. As she tugs the
drawer comes right out and the globe falls down with a sickening
crash.*

*The crash is immediately followed by a roar from the lit door
which leads to the bedrooms. It is the voice of a small man entirely
consumed with rage.*

ARTHUR (*off*). Imbecile!

LILY *picks up the globe with great calmness and puts it back on the desk, thoughtfully spinning it to find England.*

(*Off.*) Lunatic! Fool! Whatever have you ruined now! What's broken! Go on. Don't keep it from me! Confess!

LILY *picks up the drawer and carries it towards the table. She is an untidy woman, once inconspicuously good looking, whose face now wears an expression of puzzled contentment. She is wearing a lace evening dress of the late thirties, a number of straps are showing on her pale shoulders and a cigarette is dangling from a corner of her mouth. She shows no reaction at all to the diatribe from off stage.*

ARTHUR (*off*). Just try and picture me. Stuck up here. Listening, always listening while you systematically destroy. . . .

LILY *puts the drawer down on the table and knocks off a glass.*

(*Off.*) Aaah. What was that? The last of my dead mother's crockery? Speak up. Put me out of my agony. For pity's sake . . . The suspense. . . . What was it you imbecile? Side plate – dinner plate – not . . .? You're not to be trusted on your own. . . .

LILY *takes out a number of presents wrapped in bright paper and tied with ribbon and arranges them on the table. . . .*

(*Off.*) Where are they? You've hidden them again?

LILY *smiles to herself. Carefully puts out her cigarette.*

(*Off.*) Do you realize what the time is?

LILY *shakes her head.*

ARTHUR (*off*). Dusk. Have you done it? Answer me, can't you? The loneliness – of getting dressed.

LILY *puts a parcel by the place laid in the centre of the table.* ARTHUR *erupts into the room. He is a small, bristly,*

*furiously angry man. He is wearing the trousers only of a
merciless tweed suit, no collar and his braces are hanging down
his back.*

(*His anger becoming plaintive.*) You can't imagine what a fly
you are in the ointment of any little ceremony like this. . . .
How you take the edge off my pleasure in any small moment
of celebration. My own daughter's birthday. A thing I've
been keenly looking forward to and you deliberately . . .
hide . . . my . . . clothes.

LILY *puts the drawer, empty now, back in the desk and
comes back to face her husband.*

Perhaps it's a mental kink in you. Is that the excuse you'd
make? Do you plead insanity? If I had a pound for every
time you've taken a collar stud and . . . I don't know – eaten
it . . . rolled it under the chest of drawers. Now, to carefully
conceal the club braces. . . . The sort of kink that makes
women pinch things in Woolworths. Itching, destructive
fingers. Furtive little pickers.

LILY *pulls his braces, which are hanging down the back of
his trousers up across his shoulders, and fastens them. Then
she kisses his forehead. This quietens him for a moment. Then
he bursts out again.*

That's hardly the point. It's dusk.

*He runs to the windows and throws them open. A wind,
howling in, makes the candles flicker.* ARTHUR *is hauling
down the flag.*

LILY. It's bitterly cold.
ARTHUR. Found your tongue at last?
LILY. I said, it's bitterly cold.
ARTHUR (*comes back into the room, the Union Jack bundled in
his arms. He kicks the windows shut behind him*). Of course it's

bitterly cold. That wind's come a long way. All the way
from the Ural mountains. An uninterrupted journey.

LILY. Yes, I know.

ARTHUR (*folding up the flags – calm for the moment*). Think of
that. From Moscow and Vitebsk. The marshes of Poland.
The flats of Prussia. The dykes of Belgium and Holland.
All the way to Yarmouth. Just think of it. Flat as a play-
ground. That's what I tell the boys.

LILY. I know you do.

ARTHUR. It's a geographical miracle. It makes this place so
ideal for schooling boys. There's nothing like a wind from
the Ural Mountains, Bin, for keeping boys pure in heart.

LILY. I suppose not.

ARTHUR. Added to which it kills bugs.

LILY. Yes, of course.

ARTHUR. Bugs and unsuitable thoughts. You know that, Bin.
You're in charge of that side of it. Have we had a single
epidemic this year?

LILY. They cough in the night time. (*She is arranging the
presents on the table.*) Like sheep.

ARTHUR. Colds admitted. Infectious diseases not. I had a
letter only the other day. A school in Torquay. Malaria.
Decimated the boys. Brought on by the relaxing climate.
Thank heavens, Bin, for our exposed position.

LILY. Yes, dear.

ARTHUR. For heaven's sake don't complain about the wind,
then. It gets on the nerves of a saint. To have you always
carping at the wind. Think of it – one little mountain range
between here and Moscow and the boys might all go down
with malaria.

LILY. I wonder if Caroline's going to like her presents?

ARTHUR. Like her presents? Of course she's going to like her
presents. Doesn't she always like her presents?

LILY. I only wondered. . . .

ARTHUR. If you set out to make her dissatisfied. If you sow

the seeds of doubt in her young mind. . . . If you deliberately undertake to puzzle and bewilder a young girl with your extraordinary ideas of what a present *ought* to be. If you carp and criticize. . . .

LILY. I only wondered . . . if she wasn't getting on a bit for Halma.

ARTHUR. You wondered? Caroline takes it for granted. Every year she'll get her Halma and every year you'll lose three or four of her men. . . . Swallow them up like collar studs. Of course she likes Halma, you've seen her in the evenings playing it with .·. .

He puts the folded flag on top of the desk. Then shouts as he picks up the ukulele.

ARTHUR. He was here again last night!

LILY. Who?

ARTHUR. Tony Peters.

LILY. He's been here for eighteen years.

ARTHUR. But this wasn't here yesterday. He's been lurking about when I didn't know. *Singing* to you.

LILY smiles complacently downwards. ARTHUR shouts and holds out the ukulele. She takes it and holds it as if to play it. She stands still in the attitude of someone about to play the ukulele during the ensuing dialogue. The French windows open and TONY PETERS *enters. He is tall, debonair, and gay, although balding, with the cuffs of his blazer slightly fraying, his suede shoes shiny and his grey flannel trousers faded. He is carrying a string bag full of screw top bottles of light ale.*

TONY. It's bloody cold.

ARTHUR. It's you.

TONY. Of course it's me. Look here, old man. Aren't you going to dress? I mean it is Caroline's birthday.

ARTHUR. Oh my God. How far can I be goaded?

TONY (*unloads his bag, sets the bottles out on the table and then throws it on top of the Union Jack.*) I don't know. It's amusing to find out.

ARTHUR. You were here last night?

TONY. Certainly.

ARTHUR. Singing to Bin?

TONY. Keeping her company while you gave, to those few unlucky boys whose temperatures are still normal and who can still breathe through their noses, your usual Sunday evening sermon on 'Life as a stiff row from Putney to Mortlake'.

ARTHUR. So you chose that as a moment for singing . . . to a married woman.

TONY. She sat in your chair, Arthur. We turned out the lights. The room was softly lit by the one bar of the electric fire. I was cross-legged on the floor. In the half-light I appeared boyish and irresistible. Lily needs no concealed lighting to look perpetually young. From under all the doors and through the cracks of the windows the wind sneered at us from Moscow – but we didn't feel the cold. In the distance we heard you say that it is particularly under Hammersmith Bridge that God requires ten hard pulls on the oar. Above us the coughs crackled like distant gunfire. My fingers cramped by the cold, I struck at my instrument. (*He takes the ukulele from* LILY *and plays.*)

(*Singing*)   'Oh the Captain's name
             Was Captain Brown,
             And he played his ukulele
             As the ship went down. . . .'

ARTHUR. That idiotic song.

TONY (*singing very close to Arthur*).
             'Then he bought himself
             A bar of soap,
             And washed himself
             Ashore.'

LILY *puts her hand flat over her mouth like a child to stifle her giggles.*

ARTHUR. If either of you had the slightest idea of loyalty. If you had a grain of respect for me, for Sunday evening, for decent, wholesome living.

TONY (*singing*).
>   'Oh we left her baby on the shore,
>   A thing that we've never done before.'

ARTHUR. It's obscene.

TONY. Obscene?

ARTHUR. Perhaps not the words. The dirty expression you put into it. When I'm not looking.

TONY (*singing*).   'If you see the mother
>   Tell her gently
>   That we left her baby on the shore.'

The giggles explode past LILY'S *hand.*

ARTHUR. Bin!

LILY. I'm sorry. It just gets me every time. Poor baby! It's so damned casual.

ARTHUR. It doesn't seem to me a subject for joking.

LILY. But the way Tony sings it. Just as if he'd forgotten a baby.

ARTHUR. He probably has.

LILY. What can you be saying?

ARTHUR. I don't know. How can I know anything? Everything goes on when I'm not there. Furniture falls to the ground. This man sings. Crockery breaks. You pull his ears, stroke his hair as he squats there in front of you. Don't think I've got no imagination. I've got a vivid imagination. And my hearing is keen. Remember that. I warn you both. My hearing is exceptionally keen.

TONY. Hear that Lily? Stroke my hair more quietly in future.

As ARTHUR *seems about to hit him a clock groans and strikes off stage.*

LILY. Arthur. You must get dressed. It's nearly time. Caroline'll be down.

ARTHUR. Let her come down. It's time she found out something. Let her find out the lying and deceit and infidelity that all these years ... let her find out that her mother spends musical evenings breathing down the neck of an ex-night club gigolo, lounge lizard, wallflower, sensitive plant, clinging vine, baby leaving, guitar twanging, Mayfair playboy, good-time Charlie, fly-by-night, moonlight flit, who can't even do quadratic equations. Let her find out all she is. Poor girl. Poor child. You're right Bin – you've brought it on us all. She's too old for Halma now.

He sits down exhausted. They look at him in horror. He, too, is a little horrified by what he has said.

TONY. Arthur. Look here, my dear old fellow. It's Caroline's party. You wouldn't spoil a party?

ARTHUR. I don't know that I feel particularly festive.

LILY. Come on, Arthur. You know how you enjoy Caroline's birthday.

ARTHUR. I always have. Up to now. Ever since she was born.

TONY. And look Arthur, my dear old Head, I bought these for us in the pub. A whiff each after dinner.

He takes two battered cigars out of his breast pocket.

ARTHUR (*crackles and smells the cigar*). That was thoughtful of you, Peters.

TONY. I know you don't smoke them as often as one might like. Only when something a little bit festive arises from time to time.

LILY (*ecstatic*). Oh, Tony Peters! Beautifully managed.

ARTHUR. Perhaps my suspicions are unfounded.

LILY. You manage him so beautifully.

TONY. Why not finish dressing, my fine old headmaster? Let us both face the fact, you must be bitterly cold.

ARTHUR (*starts to work himself up again*). I tell you I never feel cold. Anyway it's never cold here. Only occasionally a little brisk after sunset. Anyway who's old? Didn't you tell me, Tony Peters, that in your prep school the Third Eleven Match play was once stopped by a Zeppelin? You didn't mean to let that slide out did you? What does that make you? Pretty long in bottle for a junior assistant! Ha! Ha!

TONY. I'm not a junior assistant.

ARTHUR. What are you then?

TONY. A senior assistant.

ARTHUR. You're the only assistant. I think of you as junior.

TONY (*shrugging his shoulders*). It's a fact. I give an impression of perpetual youth. (*He slaps his pocket, brings out a half-bottle of whisky.*) I thought this might slip down well with the whiffs.

ARTHUR (*mollified*). It looks like good stuff.

TONY. I've always had an eye for a piece of good stuff.

> ARTHUR *looks up suspiciously.*

TONY. Arthur, Head, do believe me. That remark was in no way meant to be offensive.

ARTHUR. I'll take your word for it.

LILY. So hurry on Arthur do. We must be just so for when Caroline comes in.

TONY. Go on Head. Spick and span. That's the order of the day. Look, Lily's in her best. As always, on these occasions.

> LILY *and* TONY *pat him, steer him towards the door; he turns to them before he goes out.*

ARTHUR. For God's sake, you two. Use your imaginations. Think what it's like being up there, wrestling with a collar in utter ignorance. Tormented. . . .

TONY. Get a start on the collar now. You'll be back with us in five minutes.

ARTHUR. Five minutes? Haven't you ever thought, Peters, the whole course of a man's life can be changed in five minutes. Does it take five minutes to die? Or catch malaria? Or say the one word to unhinge another man's wife from him? All right, I'll trust you. But look here, both. No singing. Don't torture me with that.

TONY. If I do sing, I'll sing so quietly that no human ear could ever pick it up. I'll sing in notes only audible to a dog.

ARTHUR. That's worse.

LILY. Now go on, really. Caroline can't sit and gaze at a brass collar stud on her birthday.

ARTHUR. I'm going. For Caroline's sake, I'm going. Poor child. (*He stands in the doorway, the door open.*)

TONY. For Caroline's sake. Goodbye.

> TONY *shuts the door on him. Then walks over to the basket-work chair and drops into it.*

TONY. He's not right.

LILY. About what?

TONY. About me.

LILY. What about you?

TONY. I *can* do quadratic equations.

LILY. Another year gone. Another birthday come again.

TONY. Gather all the Xs and Ys on to one side.

LILY. Eighteen years old. (*She fiddles with the presents.*)

TONY. Remove the brackets.

LILY. Oh Tony, can she possibly be happy?

TONY. Remember that minus times minus makes plus.

LILY. Tony can you hear me?

TONY. As an example. In the problem, if it takes ten barbers twenty minutes at double speed to shave 'y' tramps let 'x' equal the time taken to shave half a tramp. That's Arthur's problem. Arthur can *teach* quadratics all right. But can he *do* them. Isn't that rather the point?

LILY. Everyone here is so taken up with their own concerns.

TONY. I'm sorry.

LILY. I quite understand. You're naturally anxious for your algebra.

TONY. No, Lily. Not at all. Come and sit down.

LILY. Where?

TONY. Here. (*He slaps his knee.*)

LILY. I'd be taking a risk.

TONY. All we can take in this mean, tight-fisted world.

She giggles and sits on the floor in front of him, her elbows on his knees, gazing up at him.

LILY. Now is Caroline . . .?

TONY. What?

LILY. Happy.

TONY. She shows no signs of being otherwise.

LILY (*looks down suddenly. Her eyes full of tears*). How can she tell us?

TONY. Poor Arthur. It may not be so bad as he thinks.

LILY. When it's something we must have all noticed why don't we discuss. . . .

TONY. At first perhaps, it was our headmaster's fault. When it happened at first I blamed him. But since last birthday I've begun to suspect. . . .

LILY. Tony. You're talking about it. About Caroline. . . .

TONY (*talking quickly as if to avoid an awkward moment*). Caroline is now eighteen which must mean that she was born in 1940. Dark days with storm clouds hanging over Europe. Poor child she never knew the pre-war when you could week-end in Paris on a two-pound ten note and get a reasonable packet of cigarettes for elevenpence complete with card which could be collected towards a jolly acceptable tree gift. She never borrowed a bus and took a couple of girls from

Elstree Studio out dancing up the Great West Road and home with the milk and change left out of a pound.

LILY *begins to smile up at him.*

LILY. It's yourself you're discussing.

TONY. She missed the Big Apple and the Lambeth Walk and the Palais Glide. She couldn't even come to the party I gave for the Jubilee. Poor child, God knows I'd have invited her. Twenty-three of us in a line gliding down the Earls Court Road at three in the morning. Smooth as skaters. (*Takes up his ukelele and sings.*)

> 'She was sweet sixteen.
> On the village green.
> Poor little Angeline.'

ARTHUR (*off stage shouting*). For pity's sake.

TONY *shrugs his shoulders and puts his ukelele down, exasperated.*

TONY. Really. He's like my old landlady in the Earls Court Road. Bump on the ceiling with a broom if you so much as lifted a girl from the floor to the sofa.

LILY (*elbows on his knees*). Was it so carefree for you then, in Earls Court?

TONY (*modestly*). Carefree? Look Lily, I knew ten clubs where the drummers were happy to allow me a whirl with their sticks. I knew twenty pubs in S.W. alone which were flattered to take my cheque, and as for the opposite sex. . . .

LILY *looks at him admiringly.*

I had enough telephone numbers to fill a reasonably bulky pocket diary from January to Christmas. Even the little space for my weight and size of hat, Lily, was crammed with those available numbers.

LILY. What do you think took away all our happy days?

TONY. Are they gone?

LILY. Arthur says so. Driven away, he says, by the Russians and the Socialists and the shocking way they've put up the rates.

TONY. We can still have a good time.

LILY. But can Caroline? If she could only tell. . . .

She gets up and wanders to the table, arranging the presents.

TONY. Well there . . .

LILY. And when she never knew. . . .

TONY. Isn't that rather the point?

LILY. Deprived, Tony, of all the pre-war we ever had?

TONY. All that pre-war denied her.

LILY. What would become of us, do you suppose, if we hadn't got that pre-war to think about?

TONY (*he gets up from the chair and stands with his arm round her shoulders*). It's not all over. We don't just let it die out.

LILY. It mustn't.

TONY. We keep it going you see. And it keeps us going too.

Pause, as they stand side by side.

ARTHUR (*yelling from off stage*). What have you two got to be so damned *quiet* about?

They smile at each other and TONY *breaks away from her and walks round the room rubbing his hands and flapping his arms. He begins to talk in the clipped, stoical voice of an explorer reminiscing.*

TONY. The glass stood at forty below when we unpacked our Christmas dinner in Camp A. (*He blows on his nails.*)

LILY (*thoughtfully, softly*). I remember the day you arrived. It was summer and Arthur was out taking Cricket practice.

TONY. Frozen penguin and a mince pie which my dear sister had sent from Godalming, found, quite by chance, stuffed in a corner of my flea-bag.

LILY. I heard the sound of your two-seater on the gravel.

TONY. We broke the mince pie with our ice axes. Three dogs died in the night.

LILY. Why did you have to sell that two-seater?

TONY. . . . Prayed to God before sharing our penguin. Now a thousand miles from base camp. Had a premonition we should never see England again. . . .

LILY. I was alone in the middle of the afternoon. I heard you singing outside the window. It opened and you came in. . . . When you saw me standing all alone. . . .

TONY. Peters . . .

LILY. Yes?

TONY. With silent heroism . . .

LILY. What?

TONY. Walked out of the tent.

With a dramatic gesture he steps behind the curtain of the French window and is lost to sight.

LILY (*standing alone centre stage, her arms extended. A slight wait*). Tony! Why won't you ever be serious with me?

ARTHUR *enters, fully dressed, his hair brushed and shining.*

ARTHUR. Where the hell's he got to now?

LILY *makes a gesture of despair.*

ARTHUR. It's no use lying, Bin. I can see his filthy suede shoes under the curtain.

He pulls the curtain aside. TONY *smiles at him, pats his shoulder and walks out into the room.* TONY *lights a cigarette with great finesse.* ARTHUR *sits down at the table, raises his hands as if to say something several times. The words don't exist for what he feels that he must say.*

TONY. Now Arthur. Don't make a fool of yourself over this
ARTHUR. I . . . make a fool?

TONY. It's quite reasonable.

LILY. Tony, it seems, was discovering the North Pole.

ARTHUR. The North Pole?

TONY. Shut your eyes, Headmaster, and what can you hear? The ice cracking like gun fire in the distance. The wind howling in the guy ropes. The fizz of the solid fuel as it melts a little snow for your evening cocoa.

ARTHUR. Oh my God! (*He buries his face in his hands.*)

LILY (*laughing*). Give the poor man a little peace.

TONY. Peace? What does Arthur want with peace? He'd be as bored as a retired General with nothing to do but keep chickens and explore the possibility of life after death. As lonely as a bull without a bull fighter. As hard up for conversation as an invalid without his operation. Give him peace and you'd bury your husband. What can he listen to in this great frozen institution except the sound of his own eternal irritation? (*He claps him on the shoulder.*) Keep going, Headmaster, go off every minute. You're the dear old fog horn that lets us know we're still afloat.

LILY. Ssh. Caroline!

> ARTHUR *has raised his two clenched fists and now opens his hands and pushes himself up from the table.*

ARTHUR. She's been out for a walk.

> CAROLINE *has come in through the French window halfway through* TONY'S *speech. Now she closes them and comes into the room, crosses it, and hangs her mackintosh on the back of the door that leads to the school.*

(*Pulling out his watch and looking at it.*) She usually does at this time.

> CAROLINE *comes up to the three of them, and looks at them without expression. She sits down. The others stand. She is eighteen and extremely beautiful, her beauty being such that*

it is strange, composed and vaguely alarming. She has a look of complete innocence and wears, unexpectedly the sort of clothes worn by starlets on the covers of very cheap film magazines. These clothes have an appearance of being home made. She does not speak. While she is on the stage the other characters speak faster as if to conceal the fact of her silence from themselves.

TONY. I wonder where she's been?

LILY. Usually along the front.

TONY. She doesn't feel the cold?

ARTHUR. Brought up here, of course she doesn't notice it.

TONY. She always walks alone?

LILY. Hardly ever picks up a friend.

Pause while they all think of something to say. CAROLINE *is still expressionless.*

ARTHUR. Well – she's back just in time.

TONY. Haven't you got something to say to her?

ARTHUR. You needn't remind me. Many happy returns of the day.

He puts his hand out. CAROLINE *shakes it. Arthur sits down at the table.*

TONY. Many, many, happies, Caroline dear. (*He stoops to kiss the top of her head.*)

CAROLINE *lifts her face and kisses him on the mouth. She is still expressionless. He sits down, disconcerted, patting his lips with his handkerchief.*

LILY. Caroline, my baby. Don't grow up any more.

LILY *hugs* CAROLINE *like a child and then sits down.*

ARTHUR. She didn't like you saying that.

TONY. She didn't mind.

Pause while LILY *begins to cry.*

ARTHUR (*suddenly loses his temper*). Will you provoke me, Bin, with these bloody waterworks?

TONY. Look. She hasn't noticed her presents yet.

ARTHUR. She was upset.

TONY. No she wasn't.

CAROLINE *looks down at her place and lifts her hands in amazement. Her face is still without expression.*

LILY (*recovering*). She's seen them now.

ARTHUR (*eagerly*). She may open mine first.

TONY. Well, of all the selfish . . .

ARTHUR. She's going to. I hope you didn't notice me buying it, Caroline, in the High Street yesterday. Creeping out of W. H. Smith's.

TONY. Now you've given the game away.

ARTHUR. What are you hinting?

TONY. The mention of W. H. Smith. Now she can rule out stockings or underwear or any nice toilet water.

CAROLINE *shakes the parcel.*

TONY. Now she's guessed what it is.

ARTHUR. I don't believe she has.

CAROLINE *shakes her head.*

ARTHUR. No, she hasn't.

CAROLINE *opens the parcel, it contains a Halma set and three boy's adventure books.*

TONY. Same old things. She's bored with Halma.

ARTHUR. No she's not!

TONY. Yes she is.

ARTHUR. Anyway it's a wholesome game, Peters, unlike the indoor sports you're addicted to.

TONY. And these books! You only buy them to read them yourself. Three midshipmen stranded on a desert island. (*Picks up one and starts to read.*) 'Give over tickling, Harry, giggled his chum, little guessing it was the hairy baboon that had crept up behind the unsuspecting youngsters. . . .'

ARTHUR. She appreciates it.

LILY (*soothingly*). Of course she does, don't let's quarrel. Not on the birthday.

TONY (*putting down the book*). I suppose it takes all tastes.

LILY. Perhaps now she'll open mine.

CAROLINE *picks up a parcel.*

LILY. I made it for you, dear. It took so long. I seem to have been making it all my life.

CAROLINE *opens the parcel. A long sweater, white and endless with the school colours at the neck. She holds it in front of herself. It's far too long.*

LILY. Oh Caroline. There's too much of it. I had far too much spare time.

TONY (*putting his hand on* LILY'*s shoulder*). She likes it. She thinks it'll keep her warm.

ARTHUR. Warm? Keep her warm did you say? I tell you its perfectly warm here, all the year round.

TONY. There now, Headmaster. Lily's right. We shouldn't quarrel on the birthday. And look. She's knitted in the school colours. That'll cheer you up, you know. When you see those colours always round your daughter.

ARTHUR. At least it shows some sense of loyalty.

TONY. Of course, not being, strictly speaking, a parent my present, gets opened last.

ARTHUR (*resentfully*). A treat saved up for you.

CAROLINE *picks up* TONY'S *present. Holds it against her cheek. Listens to it.*

TONY. I believe. . . . Yes. I think I am right in saying (*radio commentator's voice*). 'The ceremony is just about to begin. It's a wonderful spectacle here to-day. The lady Mayoress has released the pigeons. The massed bands are striking up. The Boy Scouts are fainting in unprecedented numbers and . . .'

CAROLINE *undoes the parcel, produces a gilt powder compact.*

ARTHUR. What can it be?

CAROLINE *opens the compact and sprinkles powder on her nose.*

LILY. My baby. . . .

ARTHUR. Take that muck off your face. I forbid it. Go straight upstairs and wash.

TONY. Headmaster!

LILY. Surely Tony. She's still too young.

TONY *goes behind* CAROLINE, *his hands on each side of her head he directs her face to one parent, then another.*

TONY. Can you be such unobservant parents? Your daughter has now been using cosmetics in considerable quantities for many years.

ARTHUR. Is this true, Bin?

LILY. She's still a child.

TONY. Her table upstairs is covered with tubes, little brushes and the feet of rabbits. In an afternoon, with nothing better to do, she can turn from a pale, coal eyed, fourteenth wife of an oil sheik to a brash, healthy, dog-keeping, pony-riding, daddy-adoring virgin with a pillar box mouth. Her beauty spots come off on the face towels and when she cries she cries black tears.

ARTHUR. Your appalling influence.

TONY. The passage of time, Headmaster. What can you and I do to prevent it?

ARTHUR. I see her as a little girl.

TONY. Then you don't bother to look.

ARTHUR. Did *you* notice Bin?

LILY. When the sun falls straight on her I do have my suspicions. We've had so little sun lately.

> *The clock groans and strikes.* CAROLINE *puts down the powder compact and goes out of the room, through the door to the boy's department.*

She's gone.

TONY. To collect her presents from the boys.

ARTHUR. Of course. I was forgetting.

TONY. She always does that next. Then she comes back to show us what they've given.

ARTHUR. Of course . . . of course.

> ARTHUR *and* LILY *are staring thoughtfully in front of them.* TONY *walks about nervously, about to broach a difficult subject.*

TONY. My old friends. (*He gets no reaction and starts again.*) Colleagues. Of course I'm not a parent.

ARTHUR (*angrily*). If only I could be sure of that.

TONY (*smiling flattered*). Not in any official sense. But I have at least been a child.

LILY (*looking at him affectionately*). Yes, Tony, of course you have.

TONY. Now frankly speaking, isn't eighteen a bit of a cross roads? Isn't there something, can't you feel, that Caroline ought to be told?

ARTHUR. Told?

TONY. Yes.

LILY. What sort of thing, Tony, had you in mind?

TONY (*suddenly at a loss*). We must have *something* to tell her.

At least I should have thought so. Nothing to embarass any
one to tell, of course. . . . But (*more positive*) . . . her *education*.
Aren't there a few gaps there?

ARTHUR. You don't find everything in the covers of books,
Peters. That's why I always lay the emphasis on organized
games.

TONY. Yes. I noticed. (*He picks up his ukelele and begins to play
odd notes, tuning it as he speaks, more vaguely and with less
assurance.*)

> LILY *goes out and, during* TONY'S *speech, comes back with a
> tray, including a dish of sausages and mash which she puts
> down to keep warm by the electric fire.*

It's not that I'm all that keen on education myself. In fact
I merely drifted into it. It was a thé dansant on the river,
Maidenhead. The waiter was feeding the swans, he had an
apron full of bread crumbs. I was dancing with a girl called
Fay Knockbroker. She was so small and yellow and it was
hot to touch her. Like a red hot buttercup.

> ARTHUR *makes an explosion of disgust.* LILY *looks up at
> him from the dishes and smiles and goes out again.*

. . . 'Tony', she said, 'Why don't you do something? Why
don't you work?' It appeared her father Knockbroker, what
did he deal in, taps? – I really forget, has said marriage was
forbidden unless I worked. I had five shillings in my trousers
that afternoon. I couldn't have covered the cucumber
sandwiches.

ARTHUR. Grossly irresponsible.

TONY. In fact marriage, was far from my thoughts. I only
wanted to get Fay launched in a punt and pushed out under
the willows.

ARTHUR. Disgusting.

TONY. Probably. But it's that punt, those willows, that have
kept me going in all our cold winters.

LILY *comes in again with the tomato ketchup.*

That and. . . .

ARTHUR. Don't say it! I can guess. . . .

TONY. How do you live, Headmaster, without any of those old past moments to warm you up?

ARTHUR. I have my memories. A cry from the megaphone on the tow path. A cheer under Barnes Bridge.

TONY. But Miss Knockbroker wasn't stepping on board that afternoon. 'You get a job,' she said, 'or I stay on dry land and marry Humphrey Ewart. He works!'

ARTHUR (*interested grudgingly*). Did he?

TONY. She met him at the Guards' Boat Club. Blowing safes turned out to be his profession. Knockbroker was very livid when it all came out after the marriage.

ARTHUR. And you?

TONY. I went up to London to get a job. I had to leave her to pay for tea. What could I do? I didn't know anything. I had to teach. I had no great enthusiasm for education. I might have come to love it. As tutor cramming a young millionaire in the South of France, with his widowed mother bringing us long pink drinks to wash down the logarithms. . . .

ARTHUR (*suddenly roaring with laughter*). And you ended out here!

TONY. I only came temporarily. Till something else offered.

ARTHUR. You are still temporary. As far as I'm concerned.

LILY. You don't regret it Tony?

TONY (*looking round at her, then brassly*). Of course not. No regrets. I've no enthusiasm for education. But I can't help thinking. There are things Caroline should be *told*.

ARTHUR. What for instance?

TONY. We've had experience of life.

LILY (*lovingly*). Ah yes. How very true. Great experience of life.

TONY. Now, shouldn't we be passing on that experience to her?

ARTHUR. I'm against passing on experience. Boys find it very embarrassing.

TONY. But Caroline, Headmaster, isn't this rather the point we have to face? Is not, and can never be, barring all accidents, a boy.

ARTHUR. The principle's the same. I have it so often in class. You start by telling them something unimportant like the date of the Spanish Armada, 1585.

TONY. 1582.

ARTHUR. 1585.

TONY. 1582.

ARTHUR. Fifteen hundred and eighty five. The year of our Lord.

LILY. What can it matter after all these years?

ARTHUR. Imbecile. Don't interrupt me. Of course it matters. It's the mental discipline.

TONY. All right, Headmaster. Have it your own way. 1585.

ARTHUR. 1585. You start to tell them. . . . The Battle of the Armada. When England's Virgin Queen. . . . Then you've laid yourself open. . . .

TONY (imitating). Sir! What's a virgin?

ARTHUR. You see! It's most undesirable. The lesson may have half an hour to go, and if you start telling them about virgins where will you be when it's time to ring the bell? Know what I do Peters, if any questions of that type come up?

TONY. Yes. I do.

ARTHUR. I run straight out of the room and ring the bell myself. And that's my advice to you.

LILY. I suppose it's natural for them, to be curious.

TONY. They don't ask any questions unless they already know the answers.

> ARTHUR *gets up and walks about, gradually working himself into a rage again.*

ARTHUR. That's purely cynical. Their minds are delightfully blank. That's how it's got to stay, it's the only way for Caroline. You start it, Peters. You feed her with bits of geography and history and mathematics. What comes next? Little scraps of information from you about Maidenhead and the Earls Court Road. Little tips from Bin on how to make love to another man while your husband's upstairs dressing. Little hints from both of you about face powder and silk stockings, free love and Queen Elizabeth and birth control and decimals and vulgar fractions and punts under the willow tree and she'll be down the slope – woosh! on the toboggan and you'll never stop her until she crashes into the great black iron railings of the answer which, please God, she mustn't ever know.

TONY. Which one is that?

ARTHUR. That ever since you came here and met Caroline's mother this decent school has been turned into a brothel! A corrupt . . .

He stops at the sound of a baby crying off stage.

What ever?

The baby cries again.

LILY (*delighted*). A baby crying.

TONY. One of the boys has asked the right question at last.

CAROLINE *wanders in from the boys' door, her arms full of jokes. She stops by* ARTHUR *and hands him the cardboard box which, when she turns it upside down, cries like a baby.* ARTHUR *turns it and it yells. He slowly relaxes.*

LILY. It's just a joke. . . .

TONY. One of her presents from the boys.

ARTHUR. How very, very amusing.

TONY. How strange these boys are.

CAROLINE hands TONY a bottle of beer. He tries to open it and finds its made of rubber. LILY gets a squeaking banana. CAROLINE has a pair of glasses which include a nose and teeth which she puts on. They all sit down, CAROLINE quite motionless in her false nose, the others urgently talking.

TONY. Will you light the candles, Headmaster? Give a warm, shaded, Café Royal touch to the proceedings.

ARTHUR (*lighting the candles*). Sausages and mash I see.

LILY (*serving it out*). And red jelly to follow.

ARTHUR. Always Caroline's favourite men

TONY. Since she was twelve.

ARTHUR. That's why we always put it on for the birthday.

LILY. It marks the occasion.

ARTHUR. When I was a boy my birthday always fell when I was away from home at Cadet camp. My old aunt gave me my cake to take in a tin. I had to keep it under my camp bed until the day came, then I'd get it out and eat it.

LILY. Let's be grateful. Caroline doesn't have to go to Cadet camp. She can birthday at home.

ARTHUR. As often as not when I came to open that tin the bird had flown.

TONY. Poor old Headmaster. I never knew that about you.

ARTHUR. Odd thing about it. I suspected that chaplain.

TONY. Not of scoffing your cake?

ARTHUR. It's a fact. I couldn't get it out of my head. An effeminate sort of fellow, the chaplain. Welsh. And he had a sweet tooth.

LILY. I'm giving Caroline some more because it's her favourite dinner.

TONY. Yes. I see.

ARTHUR. It was terribly upsetting for a young boy in my position.

TONY. Indeed yes.

ARTHUR. You can't put your heart into Church Parade when

you suspect the padre of nibbling at your one and only
birthday present.

TONY. Let's hope you misjudged him.

ARTHUR. I was a sound judge of character. He was a man who
let the side down badly.

TONY. Suspicious of everyone. Even them.

ARTHUR. What are you trying to infer?

TONY. Nothing at all. Shall I do the honours again, Headmaster?

ARTHUR. Yes. And when you come to Caroline's glass.

TONY. What?

ARTHUR. Fill it up.

LILY. With alcohol? She won't like it.

TONY *fills* CAROLINE'S *glass. She drains it thirstily.*

TONY. There, Lily. It appears you were wrong.

ARTHUR. Thinking it over, Peters, I have thought your earlier
remarks weren't entirely senseless. Caroline *has* reached a
turning point. The time has come when she can be invited to
join her father and mother in a light stimulant. It's a
privilege, and like all privileges it brings new responsibilities.

TONY. In my humble opinion there are very few responsibilities
involved in a glass of beer.

ARTHUR. There are responsibilities in everything, running a
school, getting married, living at all. That's what we've got
to tell Caroline. She's got to have faith in something bigger
than herself.

LILY. Caroline's a woman now. Isn't that right, Tony?
Didn't you say that?

TONY. Almost a woman, I should say.

LILY. Then there are things only a woman can tell
her?

ARTHUR. There are bigger things in life than knitting patterns
and . . . bottling fruit.

I means there *are* things a person can sacrifice himself for.

The side. The school. The right comrades, sweating at the oar.

TONY. There speaks the cox of the West Woolwich rowing club.

ARTHUR. Will you mock everything Peters?

TONY. The small man yelling through a paper megaphone while the comrades lug themselves to death at forty from fatty degeneration of the heart.

ARTHUR. Is nothing to be sacred?

TONY. There are better ways of getting heart failure.

ARTHUR. It all comes down to *that*.

TONY. Caroline's young. Every day she should collect some small pleasure, to keep her warm when the years begin to empty out. She should try everything, and not mind making mistakes. When she reaches our age it won't be her mistakes she'll regret. . . .

ARTHUR. What are you telling her?

TONY. When I remember those girls at Maidenhead, their thumbs up, their faces smiling, doing the Lambeth Walk. . . . It's not the ones I got away for the weekend I regret. It's the ones I never had the courage to ask.

ARTHUR. I was trying to give Caroline something to believe in, and you will everlastingly chip in with your unsavoury reminiscences. . . .

TONY. Headmaster, are we attempting too much? Suppose we just give her some accurate information. Such as . . . where Gibraltar is.

ARTHUR. Gibraltar?

TONY. Yes. Go on. Tell her.

ARTHUR. At the bottom of Spain.

TONY. The bottom?

ARTHUR. Coming round the corner. Cadiz on the right.

TONY. You mean the right?

ARTHUR. The left then. Malaga on the right. Do I mean the left?

TONY. Headmaster. Are you sure you have any information to transfer?

ARTHUR. All right Peters. (*Getting up.*) You've managed it. You've cast a blight. You've had your mockery. You've sneered at the most respected club on the river. You've spoiled the birthday for me now. I'm not staying. It's no use beseeching.

TONY. But Headmaster.

ARTHUR. You've rubbed the bloom off the birthday for me. I'm leaving you two together. Remember – a child is watching.

He goes out slamming the door to the bedrooms.

LILY. He's gone.

TONY. Yes.

CAROLINE *sighs and sits down in the basket chair.*

TONY. If only he wouldn't take it as such a personal matter. It's not my fault where they put Gibraltar. (*He picks up the ukelele and tunes it.*)

LILY. Ssh. Caroline's expecting a song.

TONY. An old one. . . .

LILY. That Turk and the extraordinary Russian?

TONY (*singing*).

> 'Oh the sons of the prophet are hardy and bold
> And quite unaccustomed to fear,
> But the greatest by far
> In the courts of the Shah –
> Was Abdul the Bul Bul Emir.'

LILY. Of course Caroline adores this one. . . .

TONY. 'If they wanted a man to encourage the van or shout. . . .'

LILY (*shouts*). 'Atta boy.'

TONY.   'In the rear
               Without any doubt
               They always sent out. . . .'

Damn. I almost forgot. I owe the pub for those whiffs. I'm duty bound to slip back.

LILY. Oh Tony.

TONY. They were an expensive gesture. . . .

LILY. Have a look in that box. The egg money. . . .

TONY *finds five shillings in a box on the mantelpiece. Pockets it in triumph.*

LILY. Must you go tonight?

TONY (*dramatic voice stifling sobs, tough American accent*). 'I'm only a small guy, not very brave. I guess this is just one of the things that comes to a small guy and well, he's just got to go through with it if he ever wants to be able to shake his own hand again this side of the Great River. Maybe if I go through with this Lily, hundreds of little guys all over the world are going to be safe to shake their own hands and look themselves in the whites of their eyes. Maybe if I don't they won't. Kinda hard to tell. (*Looks out of the French window.*) It's just about sun up time. Guess Arthur Loudon's boys are sawing off their shot guns 'bout now down there in the alfafa. So long folks. If ma sobers up tell her Goodbye. Let's hit the trail now. Don't forget the empties. (*He hitches up his trousers, picks up the string bag of empties and lurches out of the French window.*)

LILY *is laughing hard.* CAROLINE *is quite impassive.*

TONY (*off stage*). Bang, bang, bang.

LILY. Tony, you'll kill me.

TONY (*staggering in backwards, his hand on his heart*). They killed me too, honey. Tell ma I'm feeling just fine, can't hardly notice the difference. (*Looks religiously upwards.*) O.K. Mr Gabriel Archangel. I heard you. I'm a coming. Maybe take a little time on account of this old webbed foot of mine.'

Limps out of French window.

LILY. Oh Tony Peters. What should I do without you?

Pause.

Caroline, they try to tell you things – but what can they tell you? We're not men you see, we're something different. Lots of men don't realize that. All men except, except Tony.

CAROLINE *still sits impassively.* LILY *kneels on the floor in front of her.*

LILY. I'm a woman, Caroline. And you're going to be one as well. Nothing can stop you. I'm a woman and what does Arthur call me? He calls me Bin. Bin, when my name is Lily. Now does Bin sound like a woman's name to you? You know why he calls me Bin? Because he wants me to be his friend, his assistant, his colleague, his thoroughly good chap. To rough it with him on a walking tour through life. He's said that to me, Caroline. How can I be a good chap, I wasn't born a chap. *My sex gets in the way.* That's why he gets so angry. (*She gets up and moves about the room.*) Look Caroline, do you know why he calls me Bin? Because my father did and my uncle did and so did my five brothers who all married soft hearted tittering girls in fluffy pullovers which came off on them like falling hair and white peep toe shoes and had pet names for their hot water bottles. Those brothers called me Bin. Good old Bin, you can put her on the back of the motor bike. Bin's marvellous, she can go in the dicky because her hair's always in a tangle and her cheeks are like bricks and the wind can't do her any harm, but Babs or Topsy or Melanie has to sit in front because she's such a fuss pot and so I can change gear next to her baby pink and artificial silk and get her angora all tied up in my Harris tweed. If you take Bin out it's for great slopping pints and the other one about the honeymoon couple in the French hotel, and then you can be sick in the hedge on the way because Bin's a good chap. We're women Caroline. They

buy us beer when we long to order protection and flattery
and excitement and crème de menthe and little bottles of
sparkling wine with silver paper tops and oh God, we long
to be kept warm. Aren't I right? Isn't that how we feel?
Mothers and daughters and wives. . . . (*Kneeling again.*) Oh
Caroline tell me I'm right. Caroline. Speak to us. What have
we done wrong?

> CAROLINE *says nothing, but, for the first time she smiles
> slowly and puts her hands on her mother's shoulder.* LILY
> *gets up, gets the tray which she has left leaning against the
> wall and begins to stack the plates.*

LILY. Anyway all my friends got married and there was only
Arthur. He was small and violent and believed in everything. Life wasn't much fun at home, my brothers got
married and their wives refused to take on their pets. After
the youngest left I was walking out with five Alsatian dogs.
Father economized on the wedding. 'We needn't hire a car
for Bin,' he said. My brother Tommy took me to the church
on the back of his motor bike. My first long dress and I was
rushed up to my wedding wearing goggles and waving in the
wind like a flag. We're women, Caroline. There's supposed
to be a mystery about us. We should be sprung on our men
like a small surprise in the warmth and darkness of the
night – not delivered by a boy on a motor bike like a parcel
that's come undone in the post. It shouldn't be like that for
you Caroline. The day after the marriage I told Arthur I
loved him. 'There are more important things than love,' he
said. 'What more important things?' 'Companionship,' he
said, 'helping one another. Now we're dedicated, our lives
are dedicated.' 'What to?' I asked him. 'The boys.' Can you
believe it? Those dreadful children coughing like old sheep
upstairs. I was dedicated to *them*. I went to look at them.
They were in striped pyjamas, they looked like little old
convicts with cropped heads and match-stick arms and legs.

They had hard, sexless voices and the faint, cold smell of
lead pencils. And you know what? Arthur said it would make
them think of me as more of a sport. He told them to call me
Bin. I ask you. Is that a name for a woman?

ARTHUR (*shouts off stage*). What are you doing, Bin?

LILY (*suddenly shouts back*). *Clearing away.* (*Then quietly.*) That
day was so empty. It seemed I'd been born a woman for
nothing at all. Yet I couldn't be a man. Arthur wanted me to
play cricket with the boys – can you imagine that Caroline?
My legs were still young, and his idea was to see them
buckled up in cricketing pads. My soft hands in the gloves
of a wicket keeper. . . .

ARTHUR (*off stage shouts*). I heard singing. Then the singing
stopped. What's he got round to now?

LILY. I was a woman and there was no time for me.

ARTHUR (*off stage*). Don't you realize? I went to bed because
of the way you all treated me. I can't get out again. It'd be
ridiculous!

LILY (*shouts*). I'll be up in a minute. (*Quiet.*) Just a succession
of days. Saints' Days with no lessons before breakfast. Sun-
days when the boys hit each other in the evening. Mondays
when Arthur loses his temper. Nothing. Like a party when
no one's remembered to send out the invitation. . . . Then
Tony came. . . .

> *She leaves the dishes stacked on the tray and sits near*
> CAROLINE.

ARTHUR. Bin! Come here, Bin! Don't leave me alone.

LILY. You know Tony can never be serious. Perhaps he's not
very honest. Does he speak the truth all the time? I don't
care. He treats me as if I was born to be a woman. Lily, Lily,
all the time and never a nickname. And he's made Arthur
jealous. (*Triumphant.*) *They quarrel over me Caroline. They've
been fighting over me for years.* Imagine that! Good old Bin.
She won't mind going home alone now we've met you girls. . . .

LILY *gets up. Turns to the middle of the room.*

But now it's Lily Loudon and Arthur's developed jealousy.

ARTHUR (*shouting off stage*). Are you going to rob me of my sleep? It's the semi-finals tomorrow.

LILY (*shouting*). What semi-finals?

ARTHUR (*shouting back*). Squash. Masters v Boys.

LILY (*contemptuously*). Squash! What did Tony say today? 'Lily,' always Lily you see, 'needs no half light to look perpetually beautiful.' He said that. A man with all those available telephone numbers.

ARTHUR (*plaintifully off*). The boys'll make a fool of me if I don't get some sleep.

LILY. It'll come to you Caroline. If you're a woman it's bound to come. In the middle of the afternoon, perhaps. During cricket practice. You'll hear a sound in the gravel, someone singing outside the window. You stand quite still holding your breath in case they should go away. And then, when the windows opens. . . . Caroline, I'm telling you. It's the only thing that matters. . . .

ARTHUR (*shouts*). Am I never to see you again?

LILY. One day he'll do his insides mischief, shouting like that Just put the tray in the kitchen would you. We'll wash up in the morning. I shouldn't have told you all that. I've enjoyed it though, telling myself. Don't remember it all. Only remember you're Caroline – make them call you that. Don't let them call you a funny name.

ARTHUR (*off stage*). Bin!

LILY. Coming Arthur. I'm coming now.

She looks at CAROLINE *and then goes out of the door.* CAR-OLINE *sighs, stretches and then gets up and carries the tray out of the room. The stage is empty.* CAROLINE *comes back and looks round the room. She takes out her powder compact. Standing over by the mantelpiece, powders her nose She puts out the light. The stage is dark, only the electric fire*

glowing. She draws the curtains in front of the French
window showing a square of grey moonlight. She goes and
sits down to wait. She waits. There's a footstep. She stands,
her arms outstretched.

TONY (*off stage, singing*).
        '. . . . "Do you hold life so dull.
        That you're seeking to end your career?"
        Vile infidel know
        You have trod on the toe . . .'

TONY *comes in at the French window. Stumbles in the*
darkness.

What's up? Everyone gone to bed?

CAROLINE *makes a slight sound and falls on him, her arms*
round his neck, her mouth pressed on his. In the square of
moonlit French window he is struggling to release his neck
from her hands. When he frees himself he dashes to the door
and switches on the light.

TONY. Caroline. What have they been telling you now?

She moves towards him.

Whatever it was – you can't have understood. You must
have got it wrong.

He opens the door behind him. He disappears rapidly through
the door. CAROLINE *faces the audience. She is not unduly*
upset. Her hands turn palm outwards, she heaves a small sigh,
her eyes turn upwards in mock despair. On her, the Curtain
slowly falls.

Scene Two

Early evening, the next day. The table is laid with an assortment of tea cups and plates. CAROLINE *is alone, reading a letter propped up on the tea pot in front of her. She looks very pleased, as she folds up the letter and puts it in a pocket of her skirt.*

She gets up and goes over to the roll top desk. In wrestling to get a suitcase from behind it she knocks over the globe.

ARTHUR (*shouting off stage, from the right*). What's that for mercy's sake?

> CAROLINE *brings out the battered suitcase and takes it over to the hearth rug where she opens it and begins to drop in the presents which she has arranged on the mantelpiece.*

(*Shouts.*) Bin. Is that you?

> CAROLINE *drops in the baby crier which screams in the case.*

What are you playing at you imbecile?

> CAROLINE *shuts the case.* TONY *appears outside the French windows and starts to haul down the flag.* CAROLINE *crosses the room, and, as he comes in, hastily puts her suitcase outside the door that leads to the boys' department.*

ARTHUR (*off*). Who is it, burglars? Answer me, Bin.
TONY (*folding up the Union Jack*). It may be a silly business but it pleases the headmaster. Caroline. I wanted to talk. Couldn't we talk. I promise you . . . I haven't slept. I believe, I feel sure . . . we could . . . both . . . talk.

> CAROLINE *exits through the boys' door.* ARTHUR *bursts into the room putting on his coat.*

ARTHUR. I heard you Peters. Make no mistake about that. . . .

TONY *folds up the Union Jack, puts it on the desk and goes over to the table, sits down and pours himself out a cup of tea. He looks very tired.*

TONY. I've never felt it before, Headmaster. It never really took hold of me till now.

ARTHUR. Not to speak can be just as deceptive as lying, Peters. There's an awful, deceptive silence about people in this house, a goading, tormenting, blank silence. Every question I shout is like sending a soldier into the dark night of a silent, enemy country.

TONY. Have a cup of tea?

ARTHUR. Were you in here with her?

TONY. They sat in front of me, rows of boys. Usually I feel quite indifferent about them, as if they were rows of strangers sitting opposite me in a train. I merely want to avoid conversation with them until the bell rings and we can all get out at the station.

ARTHUR. What were you two doing, banging about in here? Shall I never know the truth?

TONY. Sit down and have some tea. All that shouting must leave you parched.

ARTHUR. How can I spare my voice? Leading this sort of life, I mean.

He sits down. TONY *pours him tea.*

TONY. It's hard for you, I do appreciate.

ARTHUR. But you're the one reason for my shouting. . . .

TONY. Let me try and explain. There they sat, these children, with the pale look of old age hanging around them – of course they're much older than us, Headmaster, you do realize that don't you?

ARTHUR. Older?

TONY. And before they are finally taken away, done up in

blankets, muffled in scarves, tweed caps balanced on their ancient heads, to institutions, I felt there was something I ought to tell them. Only . . .

ARTHUR. Yes?

TONY. I couldn't for the life of me remember what it was. But if you don't tell children anything. . . .

ARTHUR. Well?

TONY. They get some extraordinary ideas.

ARTHUR. What do you mean?

TONY. I'm not sure if I'm in a position to tell you. All I can say is that I've had a shock, a pretty severe shock as it so happens, in the last twenty-four hours. I tell you, I don't often get a jolt like that these days. Last night, I say this quite frankly, sleep eluded me.

ARTHUR. Well, of course.

TONY. What do you mean, 'Well of course'?

ARTHUR. Missing Bin, weren't you?

TONY. Not at the time.

ARTHUR. I winkled her away from you.

TONY. Did you now?

ARTHUR. Brought her up to bed when you least expected it.

TONY. Oh, I see.

ARTHUR. My God, I'd liked to have seen the bewildered expression on your face when you found your beautiful bird – caged for the night.

TONY. Look, Headmaster, this shock I was referring to, it's made me think – well, I feel we shall have to face things as they are at very long last. Now I know this business has been a source of considerable interest and excitement to us all over a long period of years. It's kept us going, as you might say, when the results of the squash rackets competition and the state of the weather and the suspicion about who pinched the nail brush off the chain in the downstairs loo have been powerless to quicken the pulse. But it's gone too far, you know – we should never have started it.

ARTHUR. Of course you shouldn't. Now there's a twinge of conscience.

TONY. You know as much as I do. There's never been a breath of anything amiss.

ARTHUR (*singing bitterly*). 'Tell me the old, old, story. . . .'

TONY. It started as an occupation. Like Halma or sardines. It's kept us from growing old.

ARTHUR. Bluff your way out of it, like when the waiter comes with the bill and 'Most unfortunately my cheque book caught fire in my overcoat pocket'.

TONY. Must we go on pretending? I don't even fancy Lily. Hardly my type.

ARTHUR (*aghast*). What are you saying?

TONY. That I don't love your wife. . . .

ARTHUR. You don't?

TONY. And never have.

ARTHUR (*with quiet fury*). You unspeakable hound! (*Beginning to shout.*) You don't love her? My God, I ought to strike you Peters.

TONY. That young Fay Knockbroker remains my ideal. Small and yellow and red hot. The girl you have to keep on protecting from the wicked results of her own innocence.

ARTHUR. But Bin. . . .

TONY. Not my sort at all. A very decent, understanding sort, naturally: but the sort you'd always cram into the dicky if you had a girl like Fay to ride with in front.

ARTHUR. You don't love ·Bin?

TONY. I'm afraid not. . . .

ARTHUR. She's given you the best years of her life. . . .

TONY. Really, Headmaster . . . I feel we ought to face these facts squarely . . . otherwise . . . well it may have, perhaps it's already had . . . results we didn't foresee.

ARTHUR. Bin. Poor girl. She mustn't ever guess.

TONY (*gently*). You are . . . fond of your wife, Headmaster?

ARTHUR. Fond of her. I *love* her, Peters. When I married I

expected it would be for companionship – I'd known friendship before, Peters, genuine friendship. Someone to tramp around Wales with, to give a fill from your pouch, to share a hunk of cold Christmas pudding on a Boxing Day morning by Beachy Head – marriage is different, Peters. It takes place with a *woman*.

TONY. So I've been led to believe.

ARTHUR. And with a woman as attractive, soft, yielding, feminine as my Bin.

TONY. You take that view of her?

ARTHUR. Who mustn't ever be hurt ... Oh it's hard. I tell you that at once, Peters, to live with such a feminine person as a woman in your life.

TONY. Problems arise of course.

ARTHUR. We had our work to do. We had the school to serve. Our lives aren't ours I told her. We're dedicated to the boys. And all the time all I wanted was to stay in bed with her all day only occasionally getting up for bread and marmalade.

TONY. Really. (*A long, embarrassed pause.*)

ARTHUR. Women are sensitive creatures, Peters. Lily mustn't be allowed to guess at what you've just told me.

TONY (*gestures resignedly*). But it's led to this. . . .

ARTHUR. She mustn't be *hurt*. Lily must never be *hurt*.

Pause.

TONY. You'll perhaps resent my saying this Arthur, and that's the risk I'm bound to take. But if you don't want Lily hurt ... sometimes I'm bound to notice. . . .

ARTHUR (*proudly*). I shout at her you mean?

TONY. Well, not exactly coo.

ARTHUR. That's love. . . .

TONY. Oh yes?

ARTHUR. It takes people in different ways. Now when *you* want to make love to her I've noticed. . . .

TONY. But really!

ARTHUR. You make a joke. You pretend to be at the North Pole. You sing a song.

TONY. My weakness: I'm not serious.

ARTHUR. But when I see all that I love about my wife. The way she twists the hair over her ears when the time comes to make out a list. The soft smile she gives when no one's looking. How she shuts in laughter with the palm of her hand. . . . Then, I feel so small and angry. I see myself so powerless, so drawn into her that once I let myself go, all I believe in, all I'm dedicated to would be spent on afternoons of bread and marmalade. Then I shout. I don't know why it is. The terms of endearment I'm meaning to say just come out screaming. Is it a natural reaction?

TONY. I hardly know.

ARTHUR. And the agony of being in a room without her. The doubt and the anxiety that she'll be taken from me by the time I get back.

TONY. Really. We've got to stop it. This performance of ours has had its influence on Caroline. . . .

ARTHUR. Caroline? She's innocent of it all. She doesn't enter . . .

TONY. It has to stop, Headmaster.

ARTHUR. Who's going to stop it?

TONY. I am.

ARTHUR. You couldn't stop a catch.

TONY. I'm in duty bound. . . . (*Standing up.*)

ARTHUR. To tell Bin you don't love her. . . .

TONY. To tell the truth. For Caroline.

ARTHUR (*standing up, facing him*). Tony Peters. I need you. I know I have a sense of dedication which my wife doesn't altogether understand. In a way I'm a hard row for a woman like Bin to furrow. I shout. I'm a prey to irritation. I can't imitate snowstorms. I've forgotten all the jokes I've ever heard. She needs the bright lights, Peters, the music. The interest of another man. I knew that soon after I married her.

I can't tell you how relieved I was the day you walked through those French windows. Then I knew my married life was safe at last.

TONY (*sitting down, bewildered*). Headmaster. This is a thought I would have put well beyond you.

ARTHUR (*solicitous*). I've shocked you?

TONY. Deeply. Deeply shocked.

ARTHUR. Together, all these years, we've kept Lily so happy.

TONY. You seem, Headmaster, to have the most tenuous grasp of morality.

ARTHUR. My temper and your songs – what a crowded, eventful time we've given her. And you must confess, Peters, it's been an interest for you. I mean there can't still be so many irons in your fire these days, whatever your part in Earls Court may have been.

TONY. Oh, Headmaster. I don't know what you're trying to find, but you're getting dangerously warm.

ARTHUR. We depend on each other, Peters. You mustn't tell her. We all depend on each other. . . .

TONY. But the younger generation? What are we doing for it?

ARTHUR. Our best, Peters. Let's allow ourselves that. . . .

TONY. But when I walked through these French windows. . . .

ARTHUR. You took on a job, Peters. You can't get out of it now.

TONY. I shouldn't have been singing. That was when I made my great mistake. . . .

The kitchen door opens. LILY *enters smoking a cigarette, carrying a plate of bread and butter.*

LILY. Has Caroline had her tea? I've been cutting all this bread and butter. The trouble with living here, the butter gets as hard as the rock of Gibraltar. It blasts great holes in your sliced bread.

TONY. Don't mention Gibraltar, Lily.

ARTHUR. There you go. Trying to pretend it's cold.

LILY *drops cigarette ash on the bread, blows it off and sits down.*

LILY. Out in the kitchen I heard men's voices rising and falling, rising and falling. What've you two been talking about now?

TONY. About you.

LILY. How nice.

ARTHUR. Tony's confessed.

LILY. Confessed?

ARTHUR. What he feels about you.

LILY. What he feels. (*She looks delightedly at Tony*). Have you Tony? (*She's biting bread and butter and smoking at the same time.*) What did you say?

ARTHUR. Do you want to tell my wife, Peters? Do you want to put a stop to this whole business, once and for all?

They both look at him. TONY *gasps, smiles, and then gets up and walks up and down talking in clipped naval accents.*

TONY. 'Ladies and gentlemen. It is my duty to inform you that we have struck an iceberg. At nine-o-hundred hours, fish were noticed swimming in the first-class bath water. All ports have been alerted and in approximately ten-o-o hours they will start looking for us by helicopter. If the ship has already sunk we will rendezvous at latitude 9.700 and bob about in the water together as long as possible. . . .'

He comes to rest behind LILY'S *chair.*

Oh Lily. I can't tell you how complicated it's all become.

ARTHUR. No. You can't.

CAROLINE *enters from the boys' side, left. She is carrying her suitcase which she puts down on the floor.*

LILY. Caroline!

CAROLINE *unhooks her mackintosh from the back of the door*

and slowly puts it on. ARTHUR *and* LILY *watch her fearfully. She picks up the suitcase and stands in front of the French windows.*

ARTHUR. She's going for a walk.

LILY. Probably that's it.

TONY. Haven't you noticed the suitcase? Does she usually go for a walk with a suitcase?

LILY. Caroline. Put it down.

She gets up and goes towards CAROLINE. TONY *puts out his arm and stops her.*

TONY. Better to let her do what she wants.

LILY. What does she want? How can she tell us?

CAROLINE *opens her mouth. Long silence in which she is making an enormous effort until she says –*

CAROLINE. I want to go to London.

They look at her in amazement. In dead silence CAROLINE *puts down her suitcase.*

I've got a job with the Threadneedle Street Branch of the Chesterfield and National Bank. I start at a salary of seven pounds ten shillings a week.

She takes the letter and hands it to LILY. LILY *crying looks at it and hands it to* ARTHUR. ARTHUR *reads it and gives it to* TONY.

TONY. There seems to be some truth in what she says.

LILY. Stop her. Stop her leaving us, Arthur.

ARTHUR. She spoke. Our daughter spoke.

TONY *gives* CAROLINE *back the letter.*

CAROLINE. I have a third floor room at 109 Great Bidford Street which costs four pounds ten shillings a week, with board. I shall therefore have three pounds fifteen shillings a week left over. . . .

TONY. Caroline . . . I hate to disillusion you.

ARTHUR. She's talking. She's talking to me.

CAROLINE. Goodbye. (*She shakes* ARTHUR'S *hand.*)

ARTHUR. Forgive me.

CAROLINE. Goodbye. (*She shakes* LILY'S *hand.*)

LILY. What have we done wrong?

CAROLINE. Good-bye. (*She shakes* TONY'S *hand.*)

TONY. Good-bye.

LILY. It's too late to go now. . . .

CAROLINE. The train leaves at 7.15 from Coldsands Station. Platform One. Change at Norwich. (*She goes out and closes the French windows. For a moment she stands looking in at them through the glass. Then she disappears.*)

TONY. Let's hope she's right about that.

LILY. Why didn't you stop her?

ARTHUR (*sitting down*). She spoke to me. She said good-bye.

TONY. Well, that's right, she did.

LILY (*standing distractedly in the middle of the room*). What shall I do?

TONY. Clear away the tea.

ARTHUR. Lily. There's something you ought to know about Caroline. She hasn't said anything for a long time.

Silence. Then TONY *says.*

TONY. We'd noticed that.

ARTHUR. You didn't comment?

TONY *shrugs his shoulders.*

ARTHUR. You didn't like to?

TONY. It seemed unnecessary.

ARTHUR. Kindness held you back?

LILY. We must stop her going.

TONY. She won't meet any harm.

ARTHUR. But you don't know why she didn't speak? I told you, Peters, all the terms of endearment start shouting and screaming when I utter them. When I love someone all my love turns to irritation. I lost my temper with Caroline! I hit her! I actually hit her!

LILY (*crossing towards him*). No dear. You didn't.

ARTHUR. How do you know?

TONY. We were here in the room. You didn't hit her, Headmaster.

ARTHUR (*deflated*). I did. I wanted to hit her. After that, I thought she didn't speak. The nervous shock. Was it the nervous shock do you think, either of you?

LILY. Perhaps she didn't want to.

TONY. Or she had nothing to say to us. Although we had enough to say to her. . . .

LILY. Who shall we talk to now?

TONY. Each other, Lily. Always to each other.

LILY. Caroline! Why should she have to go, Tony?

TONY. She has to go sometime.

ARTHUR. I made her go. I hit her. I must have hit her. There's no other explanation.

TONY (*sits down in the basket-chair and picks up his ukelele*). How shall we ever know?

ARTHUR. What do you mean. For God's sake explain what you mean?

TONY. Was it your temper or her temper that stopped her speaking? Was it just the complete lack of interest that overcomes all children at the thought of the parents who gave them birth?

ARTHUR. I wasn't responsible?

TONY. What's responsible for Caroline as she is? What you told her? What you didn't tell her? The fact we told her a lie? The fact we told her the truth? Look back, Arthur. Look back, Lily do. What made us what we are? Anything our fathers and mothers said? More likely something that happened when we were all alone. Something we thought of for ourselves, looking for a passable disguise in a dusty attic, or for a path that didn't exist in the hot summer in the middle of a wood that smelt of nettles.

ARTHUR. Is that how you found things out?

TONY. My dear old headmaster. I've never found out anything. I'm not a parent, but in my weak moments, like this afternoon, I've wanted to tell things to the young. Why do we do it? Not to give them information, but to make them repeat our lives. That's all. It's finished with us and we don't want it to be finished. We'd like them to do it for us – all over again. It'll be better for Caroline to work in the bank. If only her *adding* weren't quite so shaky. Let's hope she errs, Headmaster, on the side of generosity.

LILY *gets up and begins to put things on a tray.*

ARTHUR. What are you doing, Bin?

LILY. Clearing away the tea. (*She goes out with the tray.*)

TONY (*looking at his watch*). Just ten minutes and the boys have to stop their so called 'free time' and be hoarded into prep. I shall sit with them in silence. I'm not tempted to communicate with them any more.

ARTHUR. I'd better start to get the history corrected. Then I must take the roll-call. Let's hope the boys are all . . . still with us.

He goes over to the roll top desk. Starts marking exercise books.

TONY (*singing softly*).
        'Here we sit like birds in the wilderness,
        Birds in the wilderness.
        Birds in the wilderness.
        Here we sit like birds in the wilderness . . .'

ARTHUR. Peters.

TONY (*singing*). 'Down in Demerara. . . .'

ARTHUR. Was Henry the Third the *son* of Henry the Second?

TONY. He certainly wasn't his daughter.

ARTHUR. It doesn't *look* right somehow.

TONY. I suspect him of having been the son of King John.

ARTHUR. This boy misled me!

TONY. You can't rely on *them*. Not for accurate information.

ARTHUR. Peters.

TONY. Yes, Headmaster?

ARTHUR. Bin hasn't taken it too well, Caroline going off like that.

TONY. A loss for us all, of course.

ARTHUR. It's taken a great deal from her.

TONY. Yes.

ARTHUR. It's more important than ever. . . .

TONY. What is?

ARTHUR. That we should keep going. Like we always have. If we stopped quarrelling over her now. . . .

TONY. Yes Headmaster?

ARTHUR. Think how empty her poor life would be.

TONY. And our lives?

ARTHUR. Empty too, perhaps.

TONY. You know, it must be almost twenty years ago that I came in through that window and made a joke. And now, it seems, I've got to live on that joke for ever.

> LILY *comes in. She shivers, rubs her hands and crouches by the electric fire to warm them.*

LILY. It's cold.

ARTHUR. Nonsense.

LILY. It seems strange. Just the three of us. Shall we always be alone now?

ARTHUR. There it is.

TONY. You never know. Just when you felt most lonely in Earls Court I always noticed this, it was always the time when you met a bit of new. I remember feeling damned lonely one spring evening, about this time, walking down the

Earls Court Road, and there was this beautiful girl, about eighteen, no older than Caroline in fact, her gloved finger pressed to a bell.

ARTHUR. I hope there's nothing disgusting about this reminiscence Peters.

TONY. So I said nothing. I went and stood beside her. She gave me a glance. It wasn't exactly marching orders. Then the door was opened by another girl, slightly older. 'Come in darling,' she said. 'I'm so glad you could bring your husband.' So we sat us down to four courses and later as it came on to fog, it was carte blanche of the spare bedroom for the night. You see the hostess, it all turned out, had never seen the husband.

LILY. And that poor husband?

TONY. Unexpectedly lamed that very afternoon. A taxi had run over his foot, so she explained it in the spare room.

LILY. And you walked straight up to her?

TONY. Quick work wasn't it?

LILY. A quick worker, Tony.

TONY. No grass grows under Tony Peters, thank God.

ARTHUR. I made sure that story would end up as disgusting.

LILY. Oh Tony! What adventures you've had!

TONY. Adventures, thank goodness, still come to me.

He looks longingly at LILY. *She puts an elbow on his knee and gazes into the electric fire.*

ARTHUR. Isn't the room big enough? Do you have to sit on top of one another?

TONY. Now Headmaster. It'll soon be time for roll-call.

LILY (*thoughtfully*). I haven't really had many adventures. Have you, Arthur?

ARTHUR. What?

LILY. Had many adventures?

ARTHUR (*reading*). Was that Henry II?

TONY. Was what Henry II?

ARTHUR. The chap whose son was drowned?
TONY. Drowned?
ARTHUR. In the White Ship.

> TONY *picks up his ukelele and sings to* LILY.

TONY (*singing*).
> 'Here we sit like birds in the wilderness,
> Birds in the wilderness.'

ARTHUR (*closing the exercise book and beginning to shout*). Peters.
Bin. Stop goading me both of you. Don't you even wait now
until I'm decently out of the room?

TONY (*singing*).
> 'Here we sit like birds in the wilderness,
> Down in Demerara.
>   As the ship went down.'

ARTHUR (*standing up and hitting his desk with a tremendous
crash with his fist*). Stop singing to my wife! Take your greedy
eyes off her!

> ARTHUR *and* LILY *look at each other with deep affection.*
> TONY *plays a note on his ukelele.* ARTHUR *exits.*

Curtain

A CHOICE OF PENGUINS

☐ *Further Chronicles of Fairacre* **'Miss Read'**

Full of humour, warmth and charm, these four novels – *Miss Clare Remembers, Over the Gate, The Fairacre Festival* and *Emily Davis* – make up an unforgettable picture of English village life.

☐ *Callanish* **William Horwood**

From the acclaimed author of *Duncton Wood*, this is the haunting story of Creggan, the captured golden eagle, and his struggle to be free.

☐ *Act of Darkness* **Francis King**

Anglo-India in the 1930s, where a peculiarly vicious murder triggers 'A terrific mystery story . . . a darkly luminous parable about innocence and evil' – *The New York Times*. 'Brilliantly successful' – *Daily Mail*. 'Unputdownable' – *Standard*

☐ *Death in Cyprus* **M. M. Kaye**

Holidaying on Aphrodite's beautiful island, Amanda finds herself caught up in a murder mystery in which no one, not even the attractive painter Steven Howard, is quite what they seem . . .

☐ *Lace* **Shirley Conran**

Lace is, quite simply, a publishing sensation: the story of Judy, Kate, Pagan and Maxine; the bestselling novel that teaches men about women, and women about themselves. 'Riches, bitches, sex and jetsetters' locations – they're all there' – *Sunday Express*

MORE ABOUT PENGUINS, PELICANS, PEREGRINES AND PUFFINS

For further information about books available from Penguins please write to Dept EP, Penguin Books Ltd, Harmondsworth, Middlesex UB7 ODA.

In the U.S.A.: For a complete list of books available from Penguins in the United States write to Dept DG, Penguin Books, 299 Murray Hill Parkway, East Rutherford, New Jersey 07073.

In Canada: For a complete list of books available from Penguins in Canada write to Penguin Books Canada Ltd, 2801 John Street, Markham, Ontario L3R 1B4.

In Australia: For a complete list of books available from Penguins in Australia write to the Marketing Department, Penguin Books Australia Ltd, P.O. Box 257, Ringwood, Victoria 3134.

In New Zealand: For a complete list of books available from Penguins in New Zealand write to the Marketing Department, Penguin Books (N.Z.) Ltd, Private Bag, Takapuna, Auckland 9.

In India: For a complete list of books available from Penguins in India write to Penguin Overseas Ltd, 706 Eros Apartments, 56 Nehru Place, New Delhi 110019.